# Things they never taught me

To order additional copies of
*Things They Never Taught Me,*
by
Tompaul Wheeler,
call
**1-800-765-6955.**


Visit us at
**www.reviewandherald.com**
for information on other
Review and Herald® products.

# Things they never taught me

## Tompaul Wheeler

REVIEW AND HERALD® PUBLISHING ASSOCIATION
HAGERSTOWN, MD 21740

The Review and Herald® Publishing Association publishes biblically based materials for spiritual, physical, and mental growth and Christian discipleship.

The author assumes full responsibility for the accuracy of all facts and quotations as cited in this book.

This book was
Edited by Gerald Wheeler
Copyedited by James Cavil
Cover design by Trent Truman
Cover photo by Getty Images/Darrell Gulin
Interior design by Candy Harvey
Electronic makeup by Shirley M. Bolivar
Typeset: 11/13 Bembo

PRINTED IN U.S.A.
10 09 08 07 06          5 4 3 2 1

**R&H Cataloging Service**
Wheeler, Tompaul, 1976-        .
    Things they never taught me.

    1. Youth—Prayerbooks and devotions—English.   2. Religious life.
3. Seventh-day Adventists.   I. Title.

786.732

ISBN 10: 0-8280-1978-9
ISBN 13: 978-0-8280-1978-1
Visit the author at www.tompaulwheeler.com

# Dedication

For Louis and Parp

# Contents

# Out of the Fridge, Into the Fire

## CHAPTER 1

*"Which of you fathers, if your son asks for a fish, will give him a snake instead? Or if he asks for an egg, will give him a scorpion?"—Jesus (Luke 11:11, 12).*

*"Taste and see that the Lord is good"—David (Ps. 34:8).*
*"None are so blind as those who will not see."—Modern proverb.*

*I* lived with my sister in Texas for a year, and in that time her fridge magnet collection grew by at least one: a cartoon dog-person, standing on two feet by an open refrigerator door, with the caption, "There's nothing in here that wasn't there when you looked 10 minutes ago."

OK, I make a lot of trips to the fridge, but in my defense, (a) I always take small sips and slices 'cause I'm economical like that, and (b) I need the exercise. Besides, I'm rather fond of the fridge. It's comforting and constant. Sure, it usually lacks what I'm looking for (where's chocolate milk when you need it?), but it's reliable. No one ever asks, "Hey, where'd you put the fridge after you used it?" It's a pillar of the home, quiet and unassuming. As soon as you open that door, there's the light, at your service.

One hot June afternoon at my parents' home I polished off some strawberries—so succulent, so red—and wandered back to my work. A little later I got a tad thirsty. Back in the kitchen the fridge waits right where I left it. Inside the fridge the light shines (is it ever really off?), and lo, I find a bottle of clear yet fruit-flavored drink from Food Lion. Just the ticket.

Until I taste it.

It hits my teeth, my tongue, my throat—a torrent of poison. This wasn't artificially flavored, artificially sweetened water—this was bleach. I gagged, I choked, I lunged for the sink. My mother watched in shock as my stomach heaved a splattering of thick liquid redness.

"It's . . . just . . . my . . . straw . . . berries ."

Fortunately my drink wasn't straight bleach—it was one quarter Clorox, three quarters water. My mother had mixed it to mop the floor with. It just wasn't supposed to end up in the fridge. Oops. Soon enough I was fine, and the bottle bore its own scribbled skull and crossbones, far from the foodstuffs.

Growing up, I kept hearing teachers and preachers say, "Here, drink this. It's good for you. It'll wash you clean. It'll make you right with God." Then they turned around and shut out everyone who didn't measure up to their own selective standards.

Their works-oriented potion looked like the clear water of life, but it was poison. It was bleach. While it promises purity, it burns a hole in your soul. Such religion is based on appearances, merit points, and competition with Christ—the very one who promised the woman at the well, "Everyone who drinks this water will be thirsty again, but whoever drinks the water I give him will never thirst. Indeed, the water I give him will become in him a spring of water welling up to eternal life" (John 4:13, 14).

Jesus knew those bleach peddlers all too well. One amazing thing about the

Gospel books is that they aren't just one long John 3:16 for the lost—they also combat the self-righteously smug who confuse the issues for everybody else. With one arm Jesus embraces those who sense their need of Him, and with the other He draws a line in the sand for those who think they've already got it down pat. Matthew 23 records Jesus' devastating words of woe to those who swapped God's free gifts for their own murky brew. Jesus didn't water the message down:

"Woe to you, teachers of the law and Pharisees, you hypocrites! You shut the kingdom of heaven in men's faces. You yourselves do not enter, nor will you let those enter who are trying to. Woe to you, teachers of the law and Pharisees, you hypocrites! You travel over land and sea to win a single convert, and when he becomes one, you make him twice as much a son of hell as you are. . . .

"Woe to you, teachers of the law and Pharisees, you hypocrites! You are like whitewashed tombs, which look beautiful on the outside but on the inside are full of dead men's bones and everything unclean" (Matt. 23:13-28).

One July afternoon I found myself ravenously hungry—but with no fridge access. I was in Antigua, Guatemala, on a mission trip, and a cook controlled the kitchen while I worked building a school in the blazing sun. While I had plenty of water to drink, I wanted some grub. I glanced over at a large mound of dirt, dried cement caked all over the top. In my mind's eye I saw, not a mound of dirt, but a giant frosted cupcake.

People are spiritually hungry. The problem is, that when you're starving, everything starts to look like food.

Today God's Word has been bleached. A wholistic, life-giving message has been lost in a swirl of pet verses and pet peeves. What's left is an elixir of rules and regulations, dogma and do's and don'ts, with a dash of guilt and a pinch of paranoia. When it leaves us nauseous—still hungry, still empty, still thirsty—we either give up or find something else that offers an all-too-quick fix.

And yet there's something tantalizing about it all. An all-powerful God who drops down from the sky to become a wrinkled baby, a callused carpenter, a weeping Savior sweating blood? Intrigued, I think, *That's the kind of God I'd believe in. Not one with a pointing finger, but one with His arms outstretched; not one who came to condemn the world, but one who came to save it. One who doesn't lord over us, but walks besides us. A God who narrowed the rules, yet broadened their spirit; who brings the spark of life and liberation to everyone He touches. A Holy Spirit who patiently persuades, never forcing us. A Father God who declares us no longer servants but friends, who desires us to understand Him thoroughly rather than just follow blindly and arbitrarily.*

A deity like that ought to change everything—from fixation to faith, obsession to adoration, greed to glory, hubris to humility, agony to beauty. Such a God wouldn't bleach us bland, but would bring out our true colors. And I'm here to explore with you how He does that.

We're about to dig deep. We'll talk about such topics as:

Why are some of the worst people the most religious?

What's the real deal on prophecy and the end-times?

What makes Christianity different?

What's so important about the Sabbath?

How can we know we're saved?

How can God tolerate evil?

How come God seems so different in the New Testament than the Old?

What's the meaning of sex?

How can you tell the spiritually real from the counterfeit?

"Whoever is thirsty, let him come; and whoever wishes, let him take the free gift of the water of life" (Rev. 22:17).

Dig the beauty. Ditch the bleach.

# Shuttle Launches and Pink Dolphins

## CHAPTER 2

Sailing the Amazon River between Iquitos and Caballococha (Kuh-bye-uh-coe-chuh), Peru, is a surprisingly quiet and peaceful experience, especially if the engine of your "fast boat" randomly stops three or four times midroute. I was lucky enough to travel the 200 or so miles with a group on the Ultimate Workout, a two-week summer mission project I can't get enough of. (I get to see the world, burn some calories, meet cool people, and take plenty of pictures—what more could I ask for?)

"Did you see the dolphins?" Amanda asked, leaning back in her seat.

"Dolphins? No—where were they?" I asked, standing in the aisle and peering out the windows over my friends, eyes peeled for the Amazon's legendary pink dolphins.

"They were at the last place we stopped," Amanda said. "I tried to call you so you could get a picture, but you didn't hear me."

Ah. *Well,* I thought, *that's OK—I'll just have to come back to the Amazon some-day to see some river dolphins for myself.*

Two days later I found my last flight home postponed two hours. As I waited around the Miami International Airport terminal, TV screens showed a countdown for a space shuttle launch, itself delayed a few days.

My plane was crowded, and I found myself in a window seat. I was trying to get some rest when the pilot spoke over the intercom:

"I've just gotten word that the space shuttle *Discovery* launched one minute ago. If you look out the right side of the plane, you may be able to see it head-ing to outer space."

A space shuttle launch—viewed from the air? The very idea blew my mind. Forget the dolphins—this was the true once-in-a-lifetime view. As a kid I loved all things astronomic. (A photo of the planet Saturn and one of its moons cov-ered an entire wall of my bedroom.) Unfortunately, as passengers on the plane's right side uttered "There it is!" and "I see it!" I was trapped on the left side, with multiple passengers sitting between me and the center aisle, the right-side win-dow, and the sight of a lifetime. There'd be no second chance for that. Amazonian dolphins would be easy enough to arrange sometime—spaceships from 30,000 feet, not so much.

A lot of the time, looking for God feels the same way. A certain crowd finds Him in every newspaper headline and taco, but for the rest of us God's kind of hard to spot. Sometimes He's difficult to find even in the Bible. For every John 3:16 or Psalm 23 there's something that you either trip over or ignore—stomach-churning violence, bizarre rituals, the ground opening up and swallowing people . . . Where's the Precious Moments figurine sets for those scenes?

# Things They Never Taught Me

Even in the Bible God spends much of the time offstage. While the book presents a highlight panorama of God's actions in history, it breezes over long stretches in which God bides His time and life just drones on.

And yet we're programmed for God. No matter how much we take Him for granted, forgetting Him when we need Him most, something deep inside calls out to Him. People the world over use deities as verbal filler. Profanity may not be the sincerest form of flattery, but it's inadvertent recognition of divine reality.

## Pleasing the gods

I once visited the Web site of a student who declared that "the idea of worship repulses me." Unfortunately, what's classified as worship in most religious thinking really isn't. Throughout history the superstitious have viewed the supernatural with both fear and greed. Manipulation and magical thinking rule. Drought dragging down this year's crops? Do a rain dance. Want a healthy baby? Sacrifice to the goddess of fertility. Want to win the lottery? Here are your lucky numbers for today—and be on the lookout for a charming Pisces. Send this "love gift" to my TV ministry, and you'll see a miracle. Say three Hail Marys and call me in the morning.

Most of the time religion is rootless and self-centered. Sometimes it's just silly.

The ancient Israelites' pagan neighbors never knew whether they could trust their gods. They believed that their deities needed to be coaxed and cajoled to keep sending rain and sunshine, babies and good health, lest the world fall back into the chaos from which it came. Their civilization would collapse without fertility—from the stony ground, from the womb—and they knew that they were only one bad crop season away from starvation, one generation from extinction.

In desperation their fertile imaginations concocted numerous bizarre sexual rituals to ensure that the gods remembered where crops and babies came from.

Along came Yahweh, the one true God, the great I AM, offering not magic but relationship. He turned the whole picture around when He covenanted with the ancient Israelites. The contrast with the surrounding nations was startling. Locusts eating the crops? The people would think to themselves, *Maybe we should all cut ourselves with knives.* Enemies laying the land to waste? *Perhaps only killing my firstborn will satisfy them . . .*

To a people who knew only gods who messed with their minds, impossible to perfectly please or trust, God said, *Hey, let Me spell it out for you. Here's My law. This is what you should do. You don't need to guess anymore. Just trust in Me . . . and I'll take care of you.*

"Your statutes are my delight; they are my counselors" (Ps. 119:24).

The Ten Commandments fall neatly into two parts—how we should relate to God (1-4), and how we should relate to others (5-10). In an elegant summation of ethics, God called His people to be true:

1. Be true to the God who rescued you.
2. Don't create your own false gods.
3. Don't misrepresent God with your words.
4. Remember the truth about who you are, who created the world, and why you're here by spending time with God every week on the day He set aside.
5. Be true to your family.
6. Don't kill.
7. Be true to your spouse and the vows you made to each other.

8. Don't steal.
9. Tell the truth.
10. Be true both to yourself and to others by not coveting what others have.

God promised that if His people would be true to Him and to each other, He'd be true to them. In fact, He offered the greatest deal in history: Follow Him, and He'd take them to the land of milk and honey, sunshine and money.

And instead of rituals designed to coerce the gods to do their thing, God gave His people holidays to remind them of how much He cared. Passover reminded them how God had brought them out of slavery in Egypt. The Feast of Booths reminded them of how God watched over them in their wilderness journey to the Promised Land.

Still, old habits are hard to break. The Israelites kept wandering back to false gods—gods who flattered their egos, gods who resembled themselves, gods they could park on a shelf. Even when they worshiped Yahweh, they often had the same manipulative attitude as their pagan neighbors. They thought that fervent rituals and regulations were all it took to please Him and keep the grain growing and the wine flowing—even as they dishonored God with their selfishness. God cried out to the prophet Isaiah that even their worship was rubbing Him the wrong way:

> " 'The multitude of your sacrifices—
> what are they to me?' says the Lord.
> 'I have more than enough of burnt offerings,
> of rams and the fat of fattened animals;
> I have no pleasure in the blood of bulls and lambs and goats. . . .

> Stop bringing meaningless offerings!
> Your incense is detestable to me.
> New Moons, Sabbaths and convocations—
> I cannot bear your evil assemblies. . . .
> Even if you offer many prayers,
> I will not listen.
> Your hands are full of blood;
> wash and make yourselves clean.
> Take your evil deeds
> out of my sight!
> Stop doing wrong, learn to do right!
> Seek justice, encourage the oppressed.
> Defend the cause of the fatherless,
> plead the case of the widow'" (Isa. 1:11–17).

The offerings had no meaning to God because they meant nothing to the Israelites themselves. God sighed to Isaiah, "These people come near to me with their mouth and honor me with their lips, but their hearts are far from me. Their worship of me is made up only of rules taught by men" (Isa. 29:13).

The Lord told Hosea, "I desire mercy, not sacrifice, and acknowledgment of God rather than burnt offerings" (Hosea 6:6).

## Just smite me

Still, there's a scary side to God. Most Christians ignore it, while many atheists and burned-out believers are more than happy to tell you all about it. The Bible's picture of God isn't all lambs and lullabies. Old Testament laws prescribe death for cursing your parents. Israel slaughters its enemies in cold blood—at God's command. The Lord threatens to zap Moses for failing to circumcise his sons in honor of God's covenant. Where's God's mercy in such mayhem?

Revelation describes God's judgment at the end of time, and for some it seems a little more understandable. Those future people will have witnessed good and evil in its fullness. Every one of them will have seen God revealed in the character of His followers, and to turn away from Him is to find no satisfaction in anything else. They will have made their choice. And since no life can exist without God, to pull the plug on them is an act of divine mercy.

The ancient Canaanites faced the same situation. After hundreds of years of grace God revealed Himself to them with unmistakable clarity through the Israelites. Their judgment day had come. No one could say, "What happened? I was just out getting some more popcorn . . ."

When she encountered the spies Caleb and Joshua, Rahab the prostitute of Jericho said, "We have heard how the Lord dried up the water of the Red Sea for you when you came out of Egypt, and what you did to Sihon and Og, the two kings of the Amorites east of the Jordan, whom you completely destroyed. When we heard of it, our hearts melted and everyone's courage failed because of you, for the Lord your God is God in heaven above and on the earth below" (Joshua 2:10, 11). Rahab asked that she and her family be saved. The choice was clear. And many, like her and Ruth, claimed God's mercy. But God honors our freedom of choice, and we can reject Him.

Many have asked, Is God a sadist—one who enjoys causing pain and death? The Old Testament certainly gives plenty of reasons to think so—but look at the whole picture. Perhaps we should ask, Is God a masochist—one who enjoys feeling pain? For hundreds of years He watched His children growing farther and farther from Him. And for the parts that are still incomprehensible, there is only one certain answer for now: look to Jesus. See what He is like.

In his allegory *The Great Divorce,* a tale in which citizens of hell take a bus tour to heaven, C. S. Lewis writes, "There are only two kinds of people in the end: those who say to God, *'Thy* will be done,' and those to whom God says, in the end, 'Thy will be done'" (p. 72).

**Exclusion or diffusion**

" 'Be careful,' Jesus said to them. 'Be on your guard against the yeast of the Pharisees and Sadducees' " (Matt. 16:16).

"Was Aaron allergic to yeast?"

That was my girlfriend's question as we read Leviticus 2 together. ("Every grain offering you bring to the Lord must be made without yeast, for you are not to burn any yeast or honey in an offering made to the Lord by fire" [verse 11].) Leviticus is an "odd" book—not so obscure as Nahum or Zephaniah, but pretty mind-boggling to anyone who dares enter. The swirl of seemingly random regulations, religious holidays, and priestly rites has sent many a puzzled Bible-reader running for the red letters of Jesus' words.

Yet while His red-lettered words may seem more clear, we can still learn much from Leviticus' blood-soaked paragraphs—if only for that glorious sense of recognition in the Bible's other mind-boggling passages, such as those of the book of Revelation. While it's all too easy to become numb to the eternal significance of Jesus' sacrifice, the shocking deaths of woolly lambs in Leviticus come back to us when Revelation talks about "the Lamb that was slain" (Rev. 5:12, KJV).

So why the aversion to yeast? Did Aaron need his allergy shots?

The Old Testament describes the Israelites as a "called-out people"—called out from Egypt, called to be separate, called to demonstrate purity and justice to an impure, unjust world. As "acted parables" of their special mission, God instructed them to beware of such contaminants as yeast (Lev. 2) and mildew (Lev. 13). The trouble began when their religion became little more than about being separate. As a result, despite their zeal for purity, their faith became stagnant.

The emphasis on being "called out" having fallen apart, Jesus said, "All right—I'm coming in."

And that's the model for our Christianity today. Jesus summons us to be light, shining in the darkness; to be salt, mixing in with the world, overcoming its blandness and bringing out its real flavor. That's true worship. That's representing God to a dying planet. That's our mission.

Worshipping God isn't just a one-sided exercise in stroking God's ego. As with everything else in our relationship with Him, worship is a two-way street. God is our example. We rest and restore on the Sabbath because He rested, and Jesus restored lives, on the seventh day. We love God because He first loved us. We worship God because He sent His Son to die for us. He worshipped us first . . . wholeheartedly, whole-bodily . . . in a way we can never equal or repay.

Keep your eyes open for God. Watch for Him. He's looking for you.

But if you ever see any pink dolphins headed to outer space, call me . . . and a doctor.

# Fallen Stars

## CHAPTER 3

*"It's no secret that the stars are falling from the sky*
*The universe exploded 'cause of one man's lie."—Bono,*
*"The Fly" (from the album* Achtung Baby).

*I*n 1095 Christians launched the Crusades to retake the Middle East from Islam. Untold numbers died in thousands of brutal ways. During the early twentieth century Turks slaughtered some 2 million Armenians, just to get them out of the way.

A suspect is paralyzed by bullets after reaching for a police officer's gun. Earthquakes and hurricanes swamp villages and cities. We supersize our fries while children starve on some other continent.

## The 10-billion-people question

For centuries philosophers have asked that if God exists, and God is good, why is the world so messed up? They've come up with a few different answers, such as:

A.  God is good, but He's not powerful enough to protect us from all evil.

B. God is all-powerful, but not all good (who let the mosquito onto the ark, anyway?).

C. There is no God. Remember, it's the twenty-first century—the earth isn't flat, TV's in color, and God's just an old superstition. "Believe" is just "lie" with a "be" and a "ve." This is it—for better or for worse.

D. Yeah, there's a God, but He/She doesn't really have a personality. God is just the essence of goodness—a metaphysical Santa Claus, only without the sleigh, gifts, and eight tiny reindeer. Or perhaps God is in you, and me—and that old oak tree over there.

E. Maybe there's a God. Or maybe there isn't. Life is a sexually transmitted disease and it's always fatal, so who cares anyway?

What's the answer? Why do bad things happen to good people (and, as King David asked, why do good things happen to the wicked)? What's the deal with sin? The Bible doesn't give an A-B-C answer. Instead, it tells a bit of a story—a story about a superstar whose love turned to lust.

**The bigger they are . . .**

The Bible waits until its last book to give its clearest look at the situation. The Old Testament barely mentions the devil at all. It names or suggests him in only a few places: the Garden of Eden, in heaven to needle God about Job, and a brief appearance in 1 Chronicles to tempt King David to trust in military might instead of God's power. (Second Samuel, apparently written earlier, tells the same story but with God as the tempter, suggesting that as He sought to steer Israel from false gods, He was willing to take the blame for some unseemly situations so His people wouldn't try to cover their bases by worshipping Satan, too.

Everybody around them worshiped multiple gods, and God wanted them to understand that He was the only supernatural power they should pay attention to.)

Every villain has a backstory—even the baddest sinner of them all. If anyone ever had a reason to feel special, it was the Morning Star, or, as he's called in Latin, Lucifer. Looks, love, power, health, glory—as God's top guy in heaven, he had it all.

So how did sin begin? It started when Lucifer took a stroll to the sea of glass's reflecting pool, gazed down, stroked his chin, and said to himself, "Not bad."

Slowly, subtly, Lucifer began to try to reflect a bit more glory on himself. He realized that he had only one true rival: Jesus, God's Son. If he could make his fellow angels doubt Jesus, doubt God's love and law, he could take Jesus' place in the universe, right next to God. Slowly he planted questions in heavenly minds. Were God's rules fair? Perhaps the Lord didn't have their best interests in mind? Was He holding them back from true greatness, true freedom?

The prophets Isaiah and Ezekiel tell about kings who got a little too full of themselves and, like Eve in Eden, wanted to be like God. The supernatural twists to their tales suggest that they have more than just human beings in mind. Ezekiel writes, "You were the model of perfection, full of wisdom and perfect in beauty. You were in Eden, the garden of God; every precious stone adorned you. . . . You were anointed as a guardian cherub, for so I ordained you. You were on the holy mount of God; you walked among the fiery stones. You were blameless in your ways from the day you were created till wickedness was found in you" (Eze. 28:12-15).

Satan stalks the New Testament like a lion uncaged—tempting Jesus in the wilderness, beguiling Peter to think that salvation can come without sacrifice. Later

Peter warns believers to watch out, for Satan is seeking "whom he may devour" (1 Peter 5:8, NKJV). Finally the book of Revelation pulls the picture together:

"Then another sign appeared in heaven: an enormous red dragon with seven heads and ten horns and seven crowns on his heads. His tail swept a third of the stars out of the sky and flung them to the earth" (Rev. 12:3, 4).

God fought for the universe's hearts and minds with love and wisdom. Lucifer, now God's adversary—"Satan," the slanderer; "diablo," the devil—used never-before-heard-of weapons: flattery and lies. "Stick with me and you can rule the universe," he said to one angel. "God is jealous of your cleverness," he told another. "Only I see how important you really are." Apparently he convinced a third of the angels to join his demonic posse.

"And there was war in heaven. Michael and his angels fought against the dragon, and the dragon and his angels fought back. But he was not strong enough, and they lost their place in heaven. The great dragon was hurled down—that ancient serpent called the devil, or Satan, who leads the whole world astray. He was hurled to the earth, and his angels with him" (verses 7-9).

When Jesus died on the cross, it sealed Satan's defeat. Never again would he enter heaven's exalted realm. All he can do now is cause pain, deceive many, and dog God's people in what little time he has left.

## Typical

If Lucifer's story sounds typical, you're right. The Bible tells his story again and again, only with different names in each recounting. In each case God blesses some people beyond compare, but they forget who blessed them.

In Ezekiel 16 God compares the children of Israel to a baby girl rescued from the gutter, restored to health, and raised to adulthood. God lavishes her with the finest clothes and perfume, desiring only the best for His adopted daughter. But with sapphires sparkling on her ears, leather sandals on her feet, a dress embroidered with gold, and knuckles gleaming with diamonds and rubies, Israel forgets the Father who loved her back to life. She uses every gift she received from Him to become a prostitute.

Yup, it's the same old story repeated endlessly. God lavishes blessings, beauty, and riches—on Lucifer, on Israel, on the church, on you and me—and people start thinking, *I'm hot stuff! I'm all that and a bag of manna. Yeah, God picked ME. Everybody notice ME. I've got it put together. I've got the shoes, the hair, the designer wares. Sure God says don't kill, don't steal, don't lust for Neil, but this is OK. And I'm gonna take care of myself and nobody else, so help me.*

### What's a God to do?

Imagine you're God—the most powerful being in the universe. You've created a vast variety of intelligent beings who love and honor You in perfect harmony, and You love and provide for them in return. Everybody gets along great, and everybody uses the talents You gave them to the fullest. Together everyone is creating, living, loving. But one of your top angels thinks, *Hey, what about me?*

When all is said and done, and Lucifer has made a final choice, what do you do? Do you:

A. Tell Lucifer and his followers, "Get in line today or there'll be hell to pay"? If he doesn't comply, just fry the guy.

B. Give Lucifer a complete brain-wipe and make him spend the rest of eternity on hair-counting duty?

C. Let Lucifer live long enough for his experiment with sin to play itself out completely? All of creation will witness sin's true nature and effects, see the deceiver unmasked, and make their own informed decisions to love and obey You.

If God had chosen A, all his subjects would have begun serving Him out of fear instead of love. He might have maintained their respect, but never their hearts. Not understanding the nature and consequences of sin, no one would be able to see God's justice in destroying Satan.

But if God had chosen B, He would have had loyal subjects, but no true relationship. A teddy bear may be a good listener, but it cannot love you without a mind of its own.

So God chose C. Because He values our freedom to choose. Because only by our choices can we develop character. Because devotion born of genuine love is the only devotion worth having.

Once sin hit the scene, the questions needed answers. Could God be trusted? Were His laws fair? Was sin all bad? So all could see and understand, and to settle the question of sin once and for all, the Lord decided to let sin play itself out.

Soon earth became the cosmic test-sphere. Through thousands of years the truth about Satan's lies has steadily emerged. And the universe has seen how far God's love really goes.

# A Tale of Two Adams

## CHAPTER 4

*"For as in Adam all die, so in Christ all will be made alive"*
*—Paul (1 Cor. 15:22).*

She twirled around me, her feet a blur in the green grass, sunlight a crown in her hair, juice dribbling down her chin. Then, as she grazed a hand over the tiger's head, its soft fur turned to bristles and a low, tense sound stirred in its chest.

The cat's snarl stopped our giddiness cold.

Eve froze, fists clenched on her hips. Her eyes locked onto mine, then darted from the cat to the tree.

Her face betrayed a strange mix of anger and fear.

I took an involuntary step backward, ducking to avoid whacking my head on a branch.

"Why didn't you stop me!" she hissed between her teeth.

"Is something wrong?" I asked. "I'm feeling quite fine, thank you!"

But even as I spoke the words I tasted the lie in my mouth. A shiver skidded down my spine. She flinched as I reached to touch her waist. "Don't touch me!" she yelped. With a single motion she ripped leaves from a fig tree and shaped them around her body. And together we hid, divided by sin, united by fear.

## Curses

When Adam and Eve first bit the forbidden fruit, everything seemed just peachy. Fresh possibilities exhilarated them. Then, realizing the righteousness they'd lost, they tried to make up for it through their own flimsy efforts. But the consequences of what they had done would not go away.

"Cursed is the ground because of you [Adam]. . . . It will produce thorns and thistles for you" (Gen. 3:17, 18).

Although sin would bring their death, Adam and Eve first had to live with their actions. A stubbed toe, a saber tooth, the stones piled on their son's lonely grave—all reminded them of the choice they'd made.

"And I will put enmity between you [serpent] and the woman, and between your offspring and hers; he will crush your head, and you will strike his heel" (verse 15).

"God doesn't give as good as He gets," Satan had said. "He doesn't want you to have His power, His knowledge, His status. The Lord's holding back on you." Now the universe waited to see the truth. Was God stingy? Does He give to His creation as much as He gets from them?

Breaking His law put the world under curses. Only one Person could put things right again—not by some magical spell, but by taking those curses upon Himself. God's Son would come to earth as a second Adam, to do what the first had not. Only Jesus could reverse the curses.

## Wilderness

*One Adam down, one to go,* Satan thought as he stepped onto the rock-strewn Judean ground. *This is too easy. Adam wasn't even hungry when I snared him—now Jesus is wasted from 40 days without food. The Potter will be putty in my hands—one, two, three.*

Lips chapped, skin sunburned, throat parched, Jesus looked up at the figure walking toward Him. "Did somebody say 'Son of God' back at that river?" Satan asked. "Oh—you must be starving! Here—make some bread out of these stones."

Quietly Jesus rose to His feet. A miracle? This would not be the last miracle He'd be asked to perform by someone without faith. Satan wanted Him to trust in Himself, but Jesus would trust only in the Father.

The Temple gleamed in the noonday sun as Satan and Jesus arrived on its rooftop. "Jump!" Satan urged, quoting a Bible verse promising God's protection.

Jesus pictured the scene—a man leaping from the Temple, landing unhurt among the crowd below. It'd be a smashing way to get everyone's attention and confidence. Just as Adam and Eve were impressed by a talking snake, the people would have been wowed by the miracle they'd just witnessed. But that was not the kind of attention Jesus wanted. He wanted faith given freely, out of love, not based on miracle. "It's also written, 'Don't test God,'" Jesus replied.

"Look!" Satan said from a towering mountaintop. "The whole world can be Yours—if You'll bow down to me."

Slowly Jesus shook His head. *Everyone desires a king to rule over them,* He thought, *and everyone wants to be a king themselves.* How quickly the people would turn to Him as their king, but it would be a fickle faith. With another Bible verse—"Worship the Lord your God, and serve Him only"—Jesus sent the devil packing.

Satan had tempted Him with everything he (Satan) stood for. Not satisfied with what you have? Just take more. Not happy with who you are? Grab all the attention you can get. Impatient with God's plan for you? Satan offers an easy way out. "Bow to me, and all the trials ahead will go away."

But God never takes the easy way out. If He did, He would have zapped sin and Satan in a flash. Instead the Lord followed the way of love. It's a long, hard road, one of grief, pain, and difficult choices. But it's the only road worth taking.

## It is finished

"Come down from the cross if you're the Son of God," the people demanded, but Jesus had heard it all before.

"Christ redeemed us from the curse of the law by becoming a curse for us, for it is written: 'Cursed is everyone who is hung on a tree'" (Gal. 3:13).

Thorns. Nakedness. Death. All the curses of the imperfect first Adam fell upon the perfect second. The universe watched in wonder. At last Satan's question had its answer. While Jesus hung dying on the cross, the devil was the one truly exposed—as a liar, a murderer, and a cheat.

Does God give as good as He gets? Since Satan's accusation from the branches of an ancient tree, the question begged an answer. Jesus' life and death on earth proved Satan a liar once and for all. The serpent had promised we'd become like God. Now, to reverse the destruction we'd caused, God became like us. "God just wants to rule over you," Satan had said, and so Jesus became our servant.

## Welcome back, Adam

I placed my arm around Eve's waist as we strode forward. Angels with flaming swords had barred us from Eden, but now the gates swung wide. "Eve—this is it! Do you remember—oh!"

She laughed. "Adam, you're acting as if you're two hours old!"

Suddenly we stopped in our tracks. Another had joined us. Words failed us as we dropped to our knees. At last He held out His hands to help us to our feet. "Is everything as you remember it?" Jesus asked.

"Yes," I said. I looked in wonder at His hand holding mine, and ran a finger across a scar. "Everything—except this."

# Mirror Reverse

## CHAPTER 5

*"But seek first his kingdom and his righteousness, and all these things will be given to you as well"—Jesus (Matt. 6:33).*

**M**y friend had been in my mind and prayers a lot, but the moment still startled me. Though alone, when I glanced into the mirror I saw—for an instant—not my own face looking back at me, but that of my friend.

A tilt of the earth, and then my own wide eyes looked back at me once again. I stepped back as the significance of the moment struck me. In a flash of emotion I had felt that whatever my friend might experience, might feel, I would be willing to take instead. *What form of love was this? I* pondered—this merger of casting away self and possessiveness.

The concept reverberated in my mind. A new thought struck me: Wanting to be in the place of another person may be the brightest hue of love, of selflessness—as well as the darkest shade of selfishness and hate. *How easily, I* wondered, *could darker emotions masquerade as what I'd felt.*

I saw how every emotion and motivation could be turned in on itself, yielding the opposite of what we think we intend. Such an encompassing love as I'd felt could just as easily warp into a desire to control another, benefiting only oneself. I could want to be another person to endure their pain . . . or simply for their place or power.

It's the same way throughout the spectrum of life. A flip side lurks behind every intention, with corresponding results. In lifting up a principle we forget its purpose. Ardent parenting yields estrangement. Money may buy only insecurity, and sexual intimacy may drive a couple apart. Public evangelism divorced from people's needs widens the gulf between people and God.

Check the source of your emotions and motivations. If you don't, you may find events and attitudes turning out the opposite of your expectations.

With an inverted view of the world we risk the ravages of paradox. In this distortion of reality we see only what is behind our own eyelids, and relate with others only through our own blindness. The results threaten our spirituality and our society. We forget that the quest for "godliness" originated not with Adam but with Lucifer. We make others immune to the Holy Spirit when we speak on His behalf. Moral codes misused can shatter morality. As a result we achieve what we oppose and reap what we fear.

Objects in mirror are closer than they appear.

## Magnifying fragments

They call it fundamentalism. Like so many words, such as "reckless" (which doesn't quite imply that you'll have less accidents), it's a bit imprecise. It's a term people constantly use but never quite define. What fundamentalists typically proclaim as most "fundamental" most would consider somewhere on the side—

more the fries than the burger, really; the salsa, not the burrito. (The oddest thing is fundamentalists choosing their fundamentals based on what other people *don't* believe.)

"Religious fundamentalist" brings to mind pictures of long-skirted women, long-bearded men, and their long-suffering, fun-deprived offspring. So what do I mean?

Perhaps the first word to describe fundamentalists is *fearful*. Fundamentalists fear that, without the use of force, their beliefs won't survive the barrage of competing ideas. They're convinced that their cause is right, yet fear that it will fail without extra support. All too often they'll accept any action, any attitude, no matter how degrading, if it helps ensure that their cause will prevail. Because fundamentally, they're insecure. They fail to empathize with others, because they fail to emphasize this amazing Bible promise:

" 'Not by might nor by power, but by my Spirit,' says the Lord Almighty" (Zech. 4:6).

Their terror that they'll fail unless they use force brings us to another description: *fighting*. Fundamentalists fight change. They fight the outside world. They fight against what they perceive as threatening or heretical. While they may start out as mere traditionalists, yet whatever they think threatens their identity and way of life will eventually call them to battle stations. Otherwise, they believe, if they don't give it their all, all will be lost. After all—they're doing God's work.

Fundamentalists are *selective*. They look back on eras when they imagine people were more pure, more faithful, more serious yet innocent, and pick out the details they think defined a more pure religion. Their identity is everything to them, so they emphasize the details that will most sharply define them, refine them, and bind them together—apart from and often against the world.

## In the mirror

Fundamentalists often bristle at being called such, because hey, they're only doing what's right. So sometimes it's easier to see things in a mirror. From Hinduism to Christianity to Theravada Buddhism, fundamentalist movements mimic each other, each condemning secularism, science, and modern trends, proclaiming a religion of rules and thought control.

What's the fundamental fault with fundamentalists? As they highlight specific practices, they forget the principles. They lose balance and slip into contradiction. I once knew a mother who wouldn't read any fictional books, yet raved about the latest made-up movies and sitcoms—and rarely verified the gossip she repeated about other people. Remembering a few random rules is easy. But remembering what they stood for is the hard part.

Fundamentalists' commitment is commendable, but their application needs adjustment. Worst of all, they've become unwitting idol worshippers.

To worship an idol is to reduce a reality to its reflection, yet without reflecting its reality. The image remains, but its impact is lost. What's left is an inversion that turns to perversion. God is shrunk down until He fits in a soap box.

Worshipping idols of wood and stone was a big part of why God sent His people into exile in Babylon. Afterward they finally got the point, and never worshipped idols again—not carved ones, anyway. Instead they turned everything about their religion into an idol, worshipping the symbols—the Sabbath, sacrifices, tithing, etc.—but ignoring why God gave those symbols in the first place. They forgot what those symbols stood for. The Sabbath was no longer about rest, love, and celebrating God's good work, but a day when you had to work harder—to avoid "work"—than any other day of the week. They twisted religious ceremonies that pointed to Jesus until they pointed only to themselves.

In their zeal for heaven, they lost the ability to love on earth. Jesus begged them to be balanced and focus on what *really* mattered. "You keep meticulous account books, tithing on every nickel and dime you get, but on the meat of God's Law, things like fairness and compassion and commitment—the absolute basics!—you carelessly take it or leave it" (Matt. 23:23, Message).

To twist a cliché, fundamentalists can't see the forest for all the fauna. Which is not to say that they don't believe in some very important and good things. They're just out of balance. Without the big picture, their picture of God gets distorted.

So what's the problem here? The Pharisees were plenty religious—or at least they thought they were. Isn't trying to follow God, trying to do what's right and avoid sin, always a positive—a "good thing"?

The apostle Paul came to realize that following the fundamentals by themselves won't get you anywhere. He described his fundamentalist attitudes as "confidence in the flesh" (Phil. 3:4) and said that as important as it is to be passionate, it's more vital to have a humble heart toward Jesus.

"If anyone else thinks he has reasons to put confidence in the flesh, I have more: circumcised on the eighth day, of the people of Israel, of the tribe of Benjamin, a Hebrew of Hebrews; in regard to the law, a Pharisee; as for zeal, persecuting the church; as for legalistic righteousness, faultless. But whatever was to my profit I now consider loss for the sake of Christ. What is more, I consider everything a loss compared to the surpassing greatness of knowing Christ Jesus my Lord, for whose sake I have lost all things. I consider them rubbish, that I may gain Christ and be found in him, not having a righteousness of my own that comes from the law, but that which is through faith in Christ—the righteousness that comes from God and is by faith" (verses 4-9).

Paul and his fellow Pharisees quoted the Bible and lived by the Bible, but their attitudes betrayed their actions. They loved the letter of the law, but they ignored the spirit of it. As Jesus told the Pharisees: "You diligently study the Scriptures because you think that by them you possess eternal life. These are the Scriptures that testify about me, yet you refuse to come to me to have life" (John 5:39, 40). Their Bible knowledge quiz scores would never save them—only a relationship with Jesus could do that.

The Pharisees were proud that they weren't truthless, but they were still ruthless. And that was worse.

How can what God designed for good become so twisted? It happens when people allow their own prejudices to blind them as they pick proof texts while ignoring the big picture and nuances of all Scripture. When coercion co-opts the Holy Spirit's influence. And when we use the Bible as a wedge instead of to weld.

God doesn't want us truthless, ruthless, or stuck in a life that's spiritually toothless. He wants our whole hearts, bursting forth in creative service and radiant devotion.

I've met individuals transformed by the gospel into new people with new actions and attitudes. I hope you have too. Sadly, though, I've also met those who have merely upgraded their old selfishness to self-righteousness, backed up by a selective view of the Bible. I suspect you've encountered your share of them as well.

Jesus says, "Seek Me above all, and everything else will fall into place." Fall in love with Jesus, and all the nitty-gritty will take care of itself.

# Proof in Advertising

## CHAPTER 6

*"Everything that does not come from faith is sin" (Rom. 14:23).*

*"So whether you eat or drink or whatever you do, do it all for the glory of God" (1 Cor. 10:31).*

**M**odern advertising usually boils down to two ideas:
  A. You're not good enough (implied but rarely ever stated openly).
  B. But you can be if you just buy our product.

Companies have made billions telling us we're inadequate. They've made billions more convincing us that we deserve only the best. This breath mint will get you noticed. These corn chips will make your life more fun. This beer will turn an ordinary night into a riot of good times. The key to romantic success, career fulfillment, or family togetherness is this new sports car, that hip restaurant, this new outfit. Go ahead, buy it for yourself—'cause you deserve it.

## Snake oil

The sales serpent at Lucifer's Luscious Fruits and Jams convinced Adam and Eve they were inadequate the way God had made them—but his product would take care of it. With it they'd be flashier, smarter, hipper, and happier.

It's been a winning formula ever since. Though the fruits of sin left Adam and Eve feeling less smart, less peaceful, and even less sexy, there's always the promise that the next dose will do ya. Or the one after that.

Some advertisers have a motto: "Sell the sizzle, not the steak." Don't worry about the substance of the product, they say. Just show people how exciting it is—and how exciting they'll be once they get it. Make them feel good about the merchandise—and bad about themselves if they don't have it.

Such advertisers promise to change how you feel inside by transforming you on the outside. Jesus promised exactly the opposite. He works from the inside out.

## Good and evil for dummies

The Pharisees fought evil like nobody's business—just ask them. They had right and wrong mapped out. It was OK to walk a ways on Sabbath, they said—but only so far. Watch out when grain's on your plate—lest you eat a gnat. If your teeth hurt on Sabbath, don't sip vinegar, because that would be healing yourself—but if you dip your bread in vinegar and coincidentally you feel better, so be it.

Yes, the Pharisees thought they had good and evil figured out, and they were pretty confident which side they were on. The problem was that their righteousness was all external, pinned on the outside.

As Jesus healed the sick in Gennesaret, across the Sea of Galilee, some Pharisees and teachers of the law showed up from Jerusalem. They came with a question: "Why do your disciples break the tradition of the elders? They don't wash their hands before they eat!" (Matt. 15:2). In other words, they're ceremonially unclean!

As Jesus looked into the Pharisees' hearts He thought of the selfish way they treated their families, claiming that they had dedicated their money to God, then refusing to support their parents in their old age. They used religion to benefit themselves. "You hypocrites!" Jesus exclaimed. "Isaiah was right when he prophesied about you: 'These people honor me with their lips, but their hearts are far from me. They worship me in vain; their teachings are but rules taught by men'" (verses 7-9).

Then Jesus called the watching crowd to Him. "Listen and understand," He said. "What goes into a man's mouth does not make him 'unclean,' but what comes out of his mouth, *that* is what makes him 'unclean'" (verse 10).

"Jesus!" his shocked disciples exclaimed. "Do You realize that You just offended the Pharisees?"

The Pharisees are "blind guides," He replied (verse 14). They focused on doing right and avoiding evil—but their selfishness sent them in the wrong direction.

Peter scratched his forehead. "We don't get it!" he said. "Can you explain it again?"

Shaking his head, Jesus sighed. "Are you still so dull?" he asked. "Whatever you eat goes into your stomach and leaves your body. But whatever comes out of the mouth emerges from the heart—and that's what makes you unclean. Out of your heart comes evil thoughts, murder, adultery, sexual immorality. A dirty heart is what makes a person unclean—not dirty hands" (see verses 15-20).

**Attitude is everything**

To Jesus, you aren't what you eat—you are how you think. Is your goodness on the inside, or just painted on the outside? Are your actions just to make you look good—or to help you love God and others better?

Quick—divide the following into good and evil.

love
power
money
sex
silk shirts
high grades
jewelry
new cars
cheesecake
hard work
music
trying to be more like God
Done?

Great. Then here are a few more questions. Who's more wrong: the person who believes sex is good and enjoys it with as many people as possible—or the person who believes adultery is wrong, so gossips freely about those who do it? Or who's more wrong: someone who believes in taking good care of the body, so spends many hours and dollars perfecting his or her look and figure—or those who think it's a sin to wear a pin, but serve others only when they will be noticed?

Of course they're all wrong—and right. The Sabbath is a day to rest from the stresses and obligations of everyday life. Sex is a good thing created by a good God. But everything becomes a sin when it's twisted for selfish purposes, when it's used just to make us look good in comparison to others. If something just makes us appear good on the outside, it's not helping us fill our God-given mission to love. Our goodness needs to come from the inside out.

God's rules aren't checklists for entrance to heaven—they exist to help us become the kind of people who will be happy in a place built on love. They're the fruits—not the roots—of the Spirit's work. Also they help us to love better here on earth.

**Putting the fun back in fundamentalism**

Religious fundamentalism gets all the publicity, but we're all fundamentalists when we lose sight of the bigger picture. It doesn't matter if we're a pastor, principal, pagan, or punk rock star. When we focus on something inherently good—sex, saving money, looking good, telling the truth, eating food—but forget the meaning and purpose behind it, we're off track.

To God, only two rules are fundamental: love Him, and love others. Everything we do becomes good or evil in light of those two principles.

"He has showed you, O man, what is good. And what does the Lord require of you? To act justly and to love mercy and to walk humbly with your God" (Micah 6:8).

Now, that's a plan worth buying into.

# Sellouts and Salvation Sellers

## CHAPTER 7

*"What does it profit a man to gain the whole world, and forfeit his soul?"—Jesus (Mark 8:36, NASB).*

H ave you heard their new album?"

"Oh, yeah. It's OK."

"You don't think it's any good?"

"It's not as good as their old 'indy' stuff. They're selling out. Sure, they're on the radio now, but it's just not the same."

Selling out. Everything cool seems to get morphed and messed with for mass market consumption. Out goes the edge; in comes the cash. Garfield the cat is a lot cuter and cuddlier now than in his first comic strips. Even Walt Disney's edgy, spookily whistling Steamboat Willie has become the chirpy Mickey Mouse.

And yep, even Christianity itself has gotten retooled through the years.

From their starting point smack in the middle, Christians multiplied across the Roman Empire. Greeks declared that Paul and company had "turned the world upside down" (Acts 17:6, NKJV). Within 30 years Christianity had found converts from Ethiopia to the emperor's palace.

In pagan Rome, Christians stuck out like a piñata in a pizza parlor. The multi-god-worshipping Romans viewed them as atheists for narrowing the pantheon down to one God—a deity they didn't even have images and idols for—and for not participating in the all-important state religious rituals. The bread and wine of Communion sparked rumors of cannibalism. Merchants didn't like the loss in business for their icons and magic artifacts. But the Christians' respect for life, religious liberty, and other people made them the kings of the counterculture.

**Living on love**

If the church is the bride of Christ, the church's early years were simple but romantic ones—not a lot of expensive vacations or dining out, but plenty of warm nights around the fireplace. As members of an unauthorized sect, the church owned no property, so members gathered in each other's houses or anywhere else they could find to rent.

Jesus' religion looked about to go the way of Ra or Zeus, though, when the Romans kept clamping down. Who wants to be part of a club if it means becoming part of a lion's lasagna? Was an obscure carpenter turned convict worth losing your head over?

And then Christianity won the Latin lottery.

In 306 Emperor Constantine came to power over a rotting empire. He found one way to bring the people together: religion. Constantine had grown up worshipping the sun, so why not worship Jesus, too? In fact, how about a law to make sure everybody did?

Constantine himself wasn't baptized until he was on his deathbed—he figured there's no sense rushing anything when you're just going to sin again—but suddenly the empire's persecuted were the kings of the castle, or what was left of it. The religion that had been banned was now the law of the land—but to pass with the people, it needed a makeover. While Vandals ravaged the land, new evangelists sold Christianity 2.0.

## Just folks

Around the world, "folk" religions picture the world in pretty similar ways. Most acknowledge some supreme being, but it's the lesser gods and spirits who get the rituals, images, and shrines. Christianity was about to turn folksy.

Christians used the classic "If you liked *Gone With the Wind,* you'll love *Casablanca*" formula to popularize the religion. Do you like the Greek/Roman goddess Athena/Minerva, perpetually a virgin? Meet the virgin Mary. Appreciate having a different god to turn to for every problem and situation? Meet the saints, such as Christopher, patron saint of travelers. Find it reassuring to think of your dead loved ones not just sleeping till Jesus returns (John 11:24), but already in a "better place"? We're with you there, too. Used to worshipping the sun on Sunday? Got that covered. Wish there was something more you could do to get to heaven than just trust Jesus? We've got some great bonus plans for extra reassurance. Step this way.

Thanks to Constantine, the religion of "turn the other cheek" now had the connotations of a conquering army. For the first time people found themselves forced to convert. Christianity now had power and wealth. Love of might and money inspired exclusiveness, and Jesus' law of love for God and others began to fade. Violence, a union of church and state, and the world's privileged social rankings were now acceptable and encouraged. With Christianity now relying on violent force to maintain or extend its influence, it lost the Middle East and North Africa to an ascendant Islam.

Still, the Dark Ages had its bright spots. In contrast to the rest of the world, Christians' care for the sick virtually eradicated leprosy in Europe. Monasteries preserved much written knowledge for future generations. And, um . . . castles. People lived in some pretty cool castles. Yeah, that's it.

## "I protest!"

Through the years many people spoke out against the medieval church's compromises. The most famous is Martin Luther, a German monk who found plenty to protest, from legalism to oppression of the poor. He didn't start out planning to found a new church, but one disagreement led to another, and the next thing Martin knew, he was a Lutheran.

The so-called Protestant Reformation brought a lot of changes and conflict to Christianity. Perhaps the biggest was the rejection of folk religion. Christians realized they could bypass their dead forebears and send their prayers straight to the top without shrines, statues, or anything else to aid them. (Another change, if a smaller one, was Martin Luther's moving Sunday services from sunrise to late morning to give himself time to sleep in after a long Saturday night.)

In the 1600s America became a haven for people seeking religious freedom, most famously the Pilgrims (they called themselves Separatists), who believed the Reformation hadn't gone anywhere near far enough. Rhode Island, founded by Roger Williams, was the first colony in North America to guarantee religious freedom for anybody and everybody.

The new Americans knew all too well what happens when Christians become thought police. No less an authority than President James "Father of the Constitution, or Perhaps You've Seen Me on the $5,000 Bill" Madison proclaimed, "The purpose of separation of church and state is to keep forever from these shores the ceaseless strife that has soaked the soil of Europe with blood for centuries." He and other early American leaders also knew that when religion becomes just another branch of government, most people have no more affection for church than for their local tax collector.

Still, by 1776, less than 10 percent of Americans attended church. Tired of state-sponsored religion and irritated with the Puritans, they were more than happy to do their own thing. Then, their minds free to do what they wanted, Americans rediscovered Jesus. In the early 1800s the Second Great Awakening, led by eager teachers and circuit-riding preachers, swept hundreds of thousands back into the church.

Today's religionists are eager to bring the world's governments back under the Christian banner—while, like Constantine, still holding onto decidedly unchristian values such as force, wealth, and power. But as Jesus asked: "What does it profit a man to gain the whole world, and forfeit his soul?"

Or as He might say today: "What good is it to go global if you have to sell out?"

# Self-help Religion

## CHAPTER 8

*"I am the way and the truth and the life. No one comes to the Father except through me."—Jesus (John 14:6).*

R ed strings. Holy water. Meditation. Self-help religions lurk behind the headlines, especially in the tabloids. Sometimes they sound intriguing, other times just bizarre. What's the big attraction? While self-help religion may sound fresh and new, it's really the same old same old.

## Lights, camera, transaction

Actor Tom Cruise credits Scientology for helping him reach his true potential after struggling with learning disorders. "I realized I could absolutely learn anything that I wanted to learn," he says. Cruise claims that Scientology has given him tools for living and "a larger comprehension of the world that we live in and of the spiritual being that I am."

Invented by science fiction writer L. Ron Hubbard in the 1950s, Scientology has targeted celebrities since its early years, establishing numerous Celebrity

Centers around the world. "Celebrity Center is truly an oasis in [Hollywood] for every artist on any level in their career," John Travolta told the Scientology magazine *Celebrity*. "This is an ultra-safe environment. It is the safest place in town for me. This is a place where I know I have friends I can trust."

## Can you clear me now?

Scientology promises to "clear" people of unhappiness, beginning with a free personality test that inevitably reveals the need for further assistance—at ever-steeper prices. It promises self-fulfillment and success through unique spiritual practices and counseling—and charges tens of thousands of dollars for the complete program. Scientologists use an "e-meter"—a simplified lie detector—to measure emotional trauma. They claim that Scientology can cure unhappiness—along with physical defects, such as blindness.

In the 1960s Hubbard added a new—and yet more expensive—wrinkle to Scientology's services. It seems that 75 million years ago an evil alien ruler banished billions of aliens to earth, and today we're possessed by their spirits, also known as "thetans." In order to reach the highest level of "Clear," we must banish those thetans. It'll only cost you a few grand a thetan.

Celebrity members give Scientology legitimacy and publicity, despite its small numbers. Calling itself a religion has helped protect it from charges of deception and fraud.

## Here a god, there a god

While Scientology says its philosophy is compatible with any religion, it's really a mishmash of paganism and gnosticism. Its creation story has no Supreme

Being, suggesting that we're all potential deities. Scientology rehashes a lie and a temptation first told in the Garden of Eden: We're naturally immortal, and we can achieve Godlike status and knowledge through our own efforts. It's an especially enchanting lure to someone who already feels on top of the world.

"[The serpent] said to the woman, 'Did God really say, "You must not eat from any tree in the garden"?' The woman said to the serpent, 'We may eat fruit from the trees in the garden, but God did say, "You must not eat fruit from the tree that is in the middle of the garden, and you must not touch it, or you will die."'

"'You will not surely die,' the serpent said to the woman. 'For God knows that when you eat of it your eyes will be opened, and you will be like God, knowing good and evil'" (Gen. 3:1-5).

**Garden-variety lies**

The false promises of Godhood and immortality echo through many religions, including that of the Kabbalah Centre, a worldwide organization that has attracted such celebs as Madonna, Ashton Kutcher, Demi Moore, and Britney Spears.

The Jewish mysticism known as Kabbalah dates back to the thirteenth century, but the centre's feel-good version barely resembles the original. Established in the 1960s by Rabbi Philip Berg, the organization popularizes—and, its critics say, waters down—the principles of Kabbalism. What's left is superstition—including holy water and red bracelets to ward off evil—and self-flattering promises of enlightenment and knowledge.

In his book *Becoming Like God* (now, why does that sound familiar?), Michael Berg (son of the founder) says that we can "reassemble the puzzle of creation."

We do this by seeking "the light" (and, if you're Madonna, singing about it). Berg talks of the "99 percent world" beyond our immediate senses, which we contact "during those rare moments of clarity, rapture, mystical insight, expanded consciousness, epiphany, or tuning in to pick the winning numbers in the lottery."

## Thank you, drive through

Tired of waiting on God? Berg's brand is all about putting you in the driver's seat. His Creator isn't a Father and friend—He's a vending machine. According to Michael Berg, "Kabbalah believes in a Creator, but a big difference between it and other religions is that we believe we have control of our lives. It's not 'If I do something God doesn't like, he punishes me.'" Instead, Berg's all about positive and negative energy—and manipulating reality through focusing on various Hebrew letter combos for your needs, from finding love to protection from harm. Britney Spears now has one of the "72 names of God" tattooed on her neck, a letter combination associated with "the power of healing."

The Bible introduces us to a God who watches out for us, and who says, "Before [you] call I will answer" (Isai. 65:24). He longs to hear from us—not so we can push His buttons, but out of a trust that He will supply all our needs.

## Le'go my ego

Life is full of suffering, so deal with it—no matter how many lifetimes it takes. That's the message of Buddhism, and one that actor Richard Gere embraces wholeheartedly—and with as little ego as possible.

According to a *USA Today* article, Gere meditated daily to "break down the barriers of ego." The goal, Gere says, "is to become happier . . . it's about promoting a state. And it's not an action, it's a process. . . . We're all moving away from suffering and toward happiness. We just don't know how to do it, so we mess up every time."

Buddhism believes happiness isn't found in possessions or achievement, but through letting go of self.

### Fast karma

In Buddhism what goes around comes around. Like the Kabbalah Centre's idea of negative and positive energy, Buddhism teaches that we get what we deserve. And since we keep getting reincarnated, if we can't catch a break in this life it's probably because of something we did back in the Bronze Age.

Though Jesus made clear that actions have consequences, He shattered His disciples' karmic ideas when they asked who sinned to cause a man's blindness from birth—the man or his parents. Jesus answered as He always did—with grace. "Neither this man nor his parents sinned," Jesus replied, "but this happened so that the work of God might be displayed in his life" (John 9:3). And so God ever seeks to redeem us, whether we "deserve" it or not (and the truth is, none of us never do). While Buddhism promises nirvana if we just let go long enough, Jesus offers redemption if we just let God.

### This is a test

Millions of Mormons, members of the Church of Jesus Christ of Latter-Day Saints, live in North America, including Gladys Knight and Donny and Debbie Osmond. In the early 1800s New Yorker Joseph Smith claimed to have found ancient golden tablets inscribed with the words of the *Book of Mormon*. The book purported to reveal lost truths—including that Jesus visited North America after His resurrection—and claimed to restore the gospel from post-New Testament corruption.

Like Scientology and the Kabbalah Centre, Mormonism promises its followers advanced knowledge. It begins with the idea that people originally existed as "premortal spirit beings" before coming to earth, all sons and daughters of God like Jesus. As Donny Osmond wrote on his Web site: "Our Heavenly Parents want their children to have every opportunity to receive all the blessings and privileges they enjoy. For that to happen, it was necessary for us to obtain physical bodies of flesh and bone, to come to earth and be tested on our faithfulness and willingness to keep the commandments." If we pass, we can move up the ladder to godliness ourselves—just as Jesus did.

In the words of former Latter-Day Saints president Lorenzo Snow, "Mormons believe that as man now is, God once was; as God now is, man may be." In contrast to the Bible's gospel, which urges us to "come boldly to the throne of grace" (Heb. 4:16, NKJV), Mormonism's scores of temples around the world are open only to members "in good standing." Only those deemed worthy (by yearly review) may enter.

Though the New Testament indicates that earthly temples are obsolete, Mormonism teaches that such buildings are necessary for sacred rituals and the sharing of secret knowledge. Their temples are dedicated to the doctrine of an immortal soul. Mormonism echoes the serpent in Eden, who tempted and deceived Eve with promises of divinity and natural immortality. Mormonism mixes traditional Christianity, emphasizing strong families, moral values, and hard work, with elements of gnosticism, paganism, and legalism.

**God saves those . . . who believe in Him**

While self-help religions may seem just the latest fad, they've always been around. Every false doctrine begins with the idea that we can somehow, in some way, "do it on our own." Jesus tells us just to trust in Him. Though sin has made us inherently evil and doomed us to eternal death, "God so loved the world that he gave his one and only Son, that whoever believes in him shall not perish but have eternal life" (John 3:16).

Those few words are enough to set the record straight.

# To Eros Is Human

## CHAPTER 9

*"So God created man in his own image, in the image of God he created him; male and female he created them" (Gen. 1:27).*

O f all the ways we could reproduce, sex has got to be the weirdest—and most pervasive. God could have made us genderless and had us dial up our offspring from gumball machines. Instead sexuality colors life in countless subtle ways.

It makes you carefully alternate your most flattering tops the days you have a class with *him*. Or it makes you avoid that chick who's just a little too cheery. You find yourself offering excuses for that guy who's emotionally careless but ever so cool. And just in case you didn't have enough reasons to worry about your inadequacy, it inspires those campus couples who seem to be one body with two heads, two backpacks, and maybe three arms.

We joke about it—nervously, brazenly. We rest our heads on the shoulders of parents who epitomize manhood and womanhood to us, or give us reason to think, *That'll never be me.* We flirt and flinch and flee. We admire the sharp lines of manhood, the sensuous curves of womanhood, and compare ourselves and others to ridiculous ideals.

Sexuality. It frustrates us. It inspires us. It horrifies us. It defines us. Everybody's got an opinion, but most you'd rather not hear.

One Friday morning in high school a prim and proper clinician came for an assembly. The gymnasium's huge white screen unfurled—the same screen that had brought us various comedies and dramas through the years. Suddenly it filled with images a thousand times larger than life—close-up photos of men and women's genitals disfigured by gonorrhea, chlamydia, and herpes. A stunned silence arrested my classmates. The woman spoke in a monotone, like a computer stating the weather forecast. "This is a penis with an outbreak of syphilis . . ."

Finally, mercifully, the slide show ended. Now the monologue: "Having sex," she intoned, "is like being hit by a bullet . . ."

She had a point—I think. I dunno . . . Maybe I was still too startled by all those dirty pictures. Something about irrevocability. But the violent simile stuck with me. Sex and violence have always gone together.

### Love times four

Once upon a time there were four loves. The first was *agape*. Self-sacrificing, it sought the best for everyone, judging no one, and making sure no one got left out. It looked out for the little guy, loved the lost, and soothed the sick at heart. Of all the loves it was the widest and deepest, and paved the way for all the others.

The second was *philos*—brotherly love. Like agape, it reached out to others, treating them as family. It saw the commonality in everyone, that we're all not so different after all.

The third was *storge*—affection. *Storge* loved all the quirky and endearing things, the pointy ears and grass stains and frozen raspberries. True friendship and affection, *storge* celebrated our commonalities, our differences.

The fourth was *eros*—a bubbling froth of feelings that ran circles around the others. More exclusive, yet more daring; more elusive, yet more explosive; harder to hold on to, yet more memorable. It made us feel shy, yet do crazy things. As it played tricks with our brains, it left us wondering if we had any left. Tangling our tongues, it sent our stomachs into somersaults. Demanding attention, it spurred shyness. And it sought union, integration, connection, completion.

Today eros grabs the headlines—and the imagination—as much as ever. My question is Why has sex single-handedly gotten such a bad rap—and reputation? Why not, say, food? Eating is a stronger drive than sex. We obsess on food (mmm, doughnuts . . . ooooh, chocolate). The Bible has as much to say about gluttony as fornication. The serpent used food to lure Adam and Eve into sin. Yet when was the last time you saw Christians up in arms about cheeseburgers? Why does no one picket giant billboards of burritos and fries, or boycott companies that use hunger to sell products? Surely more people, of more ages, have distorted views of food than sex. Various people have denied themselves rich foods and life's more sublime pleasures throughout the years, but the general sense has long been that sexuality's in a class by itself.

Perhaps it's because sex is such a mystery. We tread lightly around it because we so little understand it. Food is pretty straightforward—you get hungry, you grab a burrito or whip up a casserole. Voilà—satisfaction, and you live another day. Eating is vital.

Sexuality, on the other hand is optional. It's sensational. It comes with definite user instructions. Maybe something like this:

"Welcome to the world. Hope you're enjoying your fingers, toes, and earlobes. As your parents may have pointed out to anyone who cared to listen, you are a boy/girl. This detail may seem relatively inconsequential at the moment, but it'll matter later. Primary features will begin to activate in approximately 12 years, but full effects and ramifications will take several more. May require a period of adjustment. Side effects may include pain, shyness, jealousy, acne, unwanted attention, STDs, sweaty palms, insomnia, daydreaming, offspring, and ill-fitting clothing. Also may be volatile in initial years or if accompanied by indiscretion, infidelity, or insecurity. Best used within a committed, monogamous relationship sealed in the sight of God. Also best used by age 40."

## Attitude is everything

Some deeply religious people have believed that sex is only for reproduction, not recreation. Their attitude is "It's enjoyable, so there must be something fishy about it. Don't do it any more than you have to. Hey, are you gonna finish those fries?"

As I mused earlier, some people believe that sex is a good thing and have it as often as possible with as many people as they can schedule. Other people believe that getting married is a good thing—and do it as early and as often as possible. Both mind-sets are skewed. As usual, the best attitude and approach lies somewhere in between.

Christians typically take a shy approach to sex. The Bible itself is not so wary. It views sex as worthy of both respect and celebration—a true gift of God. Consider Proverbs' nuanced advice about marital faithfulness:

"Drink water from your own cistern, running water from your own well.

Should your springs overflow in the streets, your streams of water in the public squares? Let them be yours alone, never to be shared with strangers. May your fountain be blessed, and may you rejoice in the wife of your youth. A loving doe, a graceful deer—may her breasts satisfy you always, may you ever be captivated by her love. Why be captivated, my son, by an adulteress? Why embrace the bosom of another man's wife? For a man's ways are in full view of the Lord, and he examines all his paths" (Prov. 5:15-21).

Then there's the big daddy of them all, the Song of Solomon. It's not just an ode to love—it's a full-out, swooning, googly-eyed, sudsed-up block party in honor of desire, attraction, beauty, and action. Hit it, Sol and company:

> The girl:
> "Let him kiss me with the kisses of his mouth—
>     for your love is more delightful than wine.
> Pleasing is the fragrance of your perfumes;
>     your name is like perfume poured out.
> No wonder the maidens love you!
> Take me away with you—let us hurry!
> Let the king bring me into his chambers" (S. of Sol. 1:2-5).

> The guy:
> "I liken you, my darling, to a mare
>     harnessed to one of the chariots of Pharaoh.
> Your cheeks are beautiful with earrings,
>     your neck with strings of jewels.

## Things They Never Taught Me

We will make you earrings of gold,
    studded with silver" (verses 9-11).


        The girl:
"While the king was at his table,
        my perfume spread its fragrance.
My lover is to me a sachet of myrrh
        resting between my breasts.
My lover is to me a cluster of henna blossoms
        from the vineyards of En Gedi" (verses 12-14).


        The girl:
"My lover is radiant and ruddy,
        outstanding among ten thousand.
His head is purest gold;
        his hair is wavy
        and black as a raven.
His eyes are like doves
        by the water streams,
        washed in milk,
        mounted like jewels.
His cheeks are like beds of spice
        yielding perfume.
His lips are like lilies
        dripping with myrrh" (S. of Sol. 5:10-13).

The guy:
"How beautiful your sandaled feet,
    O prince's daughter!
Your graceful legs are like jewels,
    the work of a craftsman's hands.
Your navel is a rounded goblet
    that never lacks blended wine.
Your waist is a mound of wheat
    encircled by lilies.
Your breasts are like two fawns,
    twins of a gazelle.
Your neck is like an ivory tower.
Your eyes are the pools of Heshbon
    by the gate of Bath Rabbim. . . .
How beautiful you are and how pleasing,
    O love, with your delights!
Your stature is like that of the palm,
    and your breasts like clusters of fruit.
I said, 'I will climb the palm tree;
    I will take hold of its fruit.'
May your breasts be like the clusters of the vine,
    the fragrance of your breath like apples,
    and your mouth like the best wine" (S. of Sol. 7:1-9).

## Things They Never Taught Me

> The girl:
> "Place me like a seal over your heart,
>> like a seal on your arm;
>> for love is as strong as death,
>> its jealousy unyielding as the grave.
> It burns like blazing fire,
>> like a mighty flame.
> Many waters cannot quench love;
>> rivers cannot wash it away.
> If one were to give
>> all the wealth of his house for love,
>> it would be utterly scorned" (S. of Sol. 8:6, 7).

Song of Solomon presents an alluring mosaic of sexuality as vibrant, enticing, enriching, and intoxicating. The body is nothing to be ashamed or afraid of, and sexuality is a trait we should celebrate and embrace.

# Spice Is Life

## CHAPTER 10

*"Love goes toward love, as schoolboys from their books;*
*but love from love, toward school with heavy looks."*
—*William Shakespeare* (Romeo and Juliet, *Act 2, Scene 2*).

When Christians view sexuality as related only to making babies, for "procreation," they're only half right. Life isn't about sex. Sex is about life.

The Gnostics of early Christianity viewed the physical word around them as pointless compared to the heavenly realities to come. That led to two equally off-base conclusions: (a) the body is evil, so all sensory pleasure, from sex to salad dressing, must be shunned; or (b) the body is irrelevant, so it doesn't matter what you do with it.

In the beginning, of course, there was no sexuality. God said, "This is no good." In splitting the Adam, God made us in His own image, designed for relationship with others.

It's said that during the nineteenth century people were obsessed with death, but never talked about sex—at least not in "polite company." Today's Western world has shoved death's inevitability to the shadows, and we now take plenty of time to think about, talk about, and obsess about—sex. And yet, from the TV to the tabloids to the classroom, we just traffic in the trivial. Skimming the frothy surface, we focus on the frivolous, leaving our souls unfed.

So how should you relate to your sexuality—when it distracts you, diverts you, threatens to derail you? The answer is surprisingly the same for both the married and the hopelessly single: Remember the One who created you and made you a sexual being.

Eros calls us to union, to integration, to wholeness. Erotic longing expresses our natural desire to unite with what completes us. When you wake up, walk out, and space out thinking about sex, don't just slap yourself and force your thoughts to something else. Remember that emotional wholeness and satisfaction comes from many sources—spiritual, emotional, relational, social. Sexuality makes a great mask for insecurity about such issues as grades, social status, or family problems, but it's no solution.

Studies show that teens whose parents graduated from college are half as likely to have premarital sex, or engage in other risk behaviors, as the children of parents who dropped out of high school. Why the difference? It's not because parents who graduated from college all sat their kids down and said, "Don't have sex! Don't do drugs!" They just raised their kids with higher expectations, mostly unspoken. Their children are too busy living to mess around. States where residents are twice as likely to have attended college (such as Massachusetts in the Northeast, with its centuries-old emphasis on higher education) have far lower divorce rates than states where education isn't as valued, and where people are more likely to marry young, before they've begun to truly know themselves.

## The point

Eros strikes at our most contradictory desires. We daydream about intimacy, yet have nightmares about public exposure. Although we fear being found out, we long to be truly understood.

A friend of mine attended a small self-supporting Christian high school that all but forbade relationships of any sort between male and female. If someone spotted a guy and girl casually conversing more than a few times, school staff eyed them with extreme wariness and took steps to separate them.

The effect was abysmal, counterproductive to the core. Deprived of positive interaction, students started to view the complementary gender primarily as sex objects. Though the school sought to eradicate sexual tension, their policies only enhanced it. Without healthy relationships, unhealthy ones thrived—along with a climate of secrecy and suspicion.

Fundamentalist thinking sees physical action and emotional flirtation as the only ways to express and satisfy our sexual drive. Otherwise, like a puppy wetting on the carpet, our sexuality is *bad!* [cue rolled-up newspaper]. Yet that passion also points us to everything God intended for us. If you find your sexuality on overdrive, lust distracting you, examine your life. What's missing—spiritually, emotionally, relationally? What unachieved goals frustrate you? What social and familial relationships are broken? What connections does your soul really seek?

And remember the other three loves—agape, philos, storge—the building blocks upon which eros must stand. Eros cannot replace any other love by itself. Rather, eros is the frosting on the cake. Take a bowl of agape, mix in philos and storge until smooth; bake; serves two.

God created us for wholeness, for relationship. When one relational building block becomes askew, it distorts all the others, and we seek to fill in the blanks with whatever else is available. All too often eros gets asked to fill a space it was never meant to fill. Studies show that young women whose relationships with their fathers are broken are far more likely to have premarital sex than otherwise. Most extramarital affairs aren't about sex and attraction—they're about emotions faltering in the marriage. Eros by itself is no substitute for emotional wholeness. It's the fruit, not the seed; the result, not the root.

God didn't make us sexual beings just to tease us, toy with us, or test our self-control. He put that drive in us to point us to the greater completion and integration that we can only accomplish in Him.

So why the never-ending uproar about sex?

1. *Sex strikes at our identity.* Identity is core. People who don't enjoy secure identities as children of God seek identity elsewhere—as being popular, as powerful, as studly, as sexy. A study at Cornell University showed that men who felt their masculinity threatened were more likely to espouse "macho" beliefs and identify with such stereotypes. The study surveyed Cornell undergraduates, both male and female, about various social issues. As they took the test participants were randomly informed that their responses indicated either a masculine or feminine identity. Women's responses didn't change, regardless of feedback, but it significantly affected many of the men. Such "masculinity-threatened" men were more likely to support war, express homophobia, and say they'd like to buy a sport-utility vehicle (there were no increases for other classes of cars). According to the report, "masculinity-threatened men also reported feeling more ashamed, guilty, upset and hostile than did masculinity-confirmed men."

We need a healthy, wholistic sense of God and self or we'll be insecure, threatened by the actions and attitudes of others. If our identity gets rooted in our sexuality, we'll fracture on sex. But if our sexuality has its roots in our identity as God's child, we'll enjoy a well-rounded, well-founded life.

2. *Sex is powerful.* And not just because it feels so good. Frederick Buechner wrote, "Contrary to Mrs. Grundy, sex is not sin. Contrary to Hugh Hefner, it's not salvation either. Like nitroglycerin, it can be used either to blow up bridges or heal hearts" (*Wishful Thinking: A Theological ABC,* p. 87).

3. *God created sexuality to point us to Him.* The mystery of our sexuality is wrapped up in this: God created us in His "own image," "male and female," so our sexuality, in unity, is designed to reflect Him. Sexuality is holy. The Bible describes the marital bond as male and female joined in "one flesh." In God's ideal, two people unite emotionally, spiritually, and—sometimes literally—physically. As Genesis 2:24 describes it: "Therefore shall a man leave his father and his mother, and shall cleave unto his wife: and they shall be one flesh" (KJV).

The Hebrew word for "cleave" means "to adhere closely," like two sheets of paper glued together. It may be possible to pull the two sheets apart, but not without damage to them both. God designed sexual relations to bring us together in a unity that points to Him. That's part of the power and meaning behind sex.

4. *Sex involves relationship.* We're born to bond—parents and offspring, friends and family. If we don't have healthy bonds with others, especially our parents and family, we'll have a much harder time forging an intimate sexual bond that lasts a lifetime.

**Born to bond**

Anthropologist Desmond Morris defined the stages of intimate pair bonding in 12 general steps.

1. Eye to body
2. Eye to eye
3. Voice to voice
4. Hand to hand (or shoulder)
5. Arm to shoulder
6. Arm to waist
7. Mouth to mouth
8. Hand to head/face
9. Hand to body
10. Mouth to breast
11. Hand to genitals
12. Intercourse—body to body, soul to soul

For healthy bonding, the steps must occur in order, and nothing should rush them. Such a process, designed by God, creates a powerful connection that lasts a lifetime.

Sex is the fruit of love, but we should not confuse it with love itself. Like legalists who focus on doing the right things to get to heaven instead of focusing on their relationship with God, people confuse sex with love. *(He must love me—I mean, he had sex with me . . .)* A relationship built on sex is a house of cards. But sex built on a lifetime relationship is a house of delights.

How should we relate to sex? With patience, love, and respect. In other words, with grace.

## Hold your tongue

The ancient city of Corinth had a pretty racy reputation—so much so that "Corinthian girl" was slang for "prostitute." Hundreds of temple prostitutes helped locals observe the community religion. Corinth's first Christians faced ruining Christianity's reputation either by backsliding into even greater immorality or by distorting the gospel through self-righteous condemnation of outsiders. Paul told them that when it came to sex, they should shape up inside the church community, and shut up about it to outsiders. He wrote:

"I have written you in my letter not to associate with sexually immoral people—not at all meaning the people of this world who are immoral, or the greedy and swindlers, or idolaters. In that case you would have to leave this world. But now I am writing you that you must not associate with anyone who calls himself a brother but is sexually immoral or greedy, an idolater or a slanderer, a drunkard or a swindler. With such a man do not even eat. *What business is it of mine to judge those outside the church? Are you not to judge those inside? God will judge those outside*" (1 Cor. 5:9-13).

Paul told them always to be friends with people outside the church, never judgmental. Unfortunately, one of the biggest things today's Christians are known for is exactly what the apostle told them *not* to do: lecturing the outside world about sex. Countless Christian ministries and messengers would have to change their focus and attitudes radically if they took Paul's advice seriously. Christians who focus their attitudes and energies condemning the sexual lifestyles of people outside the church do a great harm to the gospel. Ignoring Paul's advice to mind the church's own business, they harden their hearts to God. The Lord wants us to live holy, complete, abundant, joyful lives that give Him glory and attract people who want what they see we have. Wasting time condemning other people's choices for not measuring up only fogs our witness, and repels those we might otherwise reach. It's counterproductive in the extreme.

Too many Christians view sexuality as a necessary evil. It seems to me that it's an unnecessary blessing. Enjoy it as God designed it.

# Grace

## CHAPTER 11

*"Then one of the seraphs flew to me with a live coal in his hand, which he had taken with tongs from the altar. With it he touched my mouth and said, 'See, this has touched your lips; your guilt is taken away and your sin atoned for'" (Isa. 6:6, 7).*

*G*race is a sticky subject.

People *like* grace, or at least the idea of it—amazing grace, God shed His grace on thee—but usually only when they're the ones receiving it. Most of the time, though, we're just not that fond of it. Take our man Jonah, of fish digestion fame. God asked him to preach doom to his country's enemies—a potentially fun assignment, true, but not if it meant rubbing shoulders with (and risking quick murder from) a bunch of filthy pagans. Spared from drowning by a big-tongued life raft—and a big heap of God's grace—Jonah declared "Repent or die" with relish. When Nineveh chose option A and God spared the sinful city, the prophet threw a pity party and begged to die himself. "I knew You'd do this!" he snapped at Yahweh. "I knew it! This is so like You—gracious and compassionate, slow to anger and abounding in love, a God who relents from sending calamity."

Grace can be offensive. Controversial. Even scandalous. Doesn't grace make goodness too easy to flout? Doesn't a spoonful of guilt make the righteousness go down better?

The reaction is predictable. I remember a dozen arguments about pregnant teenagers—should churches throw them baby showers? Isn't that just *encouraging* teens to get pregnant—or, even worse, have sex? I can hear the cell phone conversation: "Janet, Tony says I'm beautiful, and sex is beautiful—and besides, did you see those cute baby clothes Wendy got?"

Every time I heard those discussions, I wondered. If the faceless girls had gotten support and encouragement from their church families—from any family— beforehand, maybe they would have been a little less likely to get pregnant at all.

Such wary attitudes toward grace pop up even in politics. When scientists produced a vaccine for the HPV virus, which causes cervical cancer, conservative activists spoke against it. If all young girls got themselves vaccinated against the sexually transmitted disease, they reasoned, wouldn't they be more tempted to dabble in sex without the fear of additional consequences? After all, isn't guilt a greater motivator than grace?

And sometimes I wonder—what good is grace, anyway? It asks so much. It works so slow. Sometimes I question, *Is evil more powerful than grace?* Take, for example, Kathleen Ham's story.

### Scorched

Young and single, Kathleen Ham let life take her where it would. A former University of California at Berkeley student, she considered herself up to handling anything. In 1968 reports of the Prague student uprising inspired her to hitchhike to Czechoslovakia to check things out for herself. *This is history,* she thought to herself. *I have to see it.* Her future looked bright and carefree.

But on June 26, 1973, Ms. Ham's life changed forever, thanks to an evil that never even showed its face.

That night she was alone, asleep, at a friend's apartment, having just moved to Manhattan. A noise awoke her. Through the darkness she spotted a shoe on the fire escape, a man's hand on a window. Suddenly the window was open, a sheet over her head, and a serrated knife scratching her throat. Her screams seemed to come from somewhere outside herself. She fought, but she could not resist his assault. A neighbor heard her screams and called 911.

"When I saw I was still alive, I was disappointed," Kathleen Ham would later remember to reporters. Meanwhile police caught a suspect, Fletcher Anderson Worrell, on the street, and had Ms. Ham look at him. "I don't know, I don't know," she said, because he'd not let her see his face.

The doctor who examined her found it hard to believe that she'd been raped, for she seemed too calm. The trial was a travesty, as in 1973 the law required proof of physical force. The rapist's defense lawyer cross-examined Ms. Ham for a day and a half. Had she been a virgin? Was she, perhaps, a prostitute who had rough sex with a pimp? And why hadn't she just run away, the lawyer demanded. "Were both your legs broken?"

A split jury let Fletcher Anderson Worrell go free. On October 31, 1975, a court convicted Worrell of yet another assault, but in October 1976 a legal loophole set him loose again.

Meanwhile Ms. Ham struggled to rebuild her shattered life. Insomnia stalked her nights, and she found it impossible to sleep more than a handful of hours. She insisted on leaving an exit door unlocked wherever she stayed, and she shied away from physical contact or getting too close to anyone. "I just didn't want to be kissed," Ms. Ham said. "I didn't like to be touched by strangers." She became a civil rights lawyer in California, but a sudden phobia in the early 1990s kept her from entering a courtroom, and to cope with life she became a chain-smoker.

After a decade in Egypt, Worrell returned to the United States in the early 2000s. In May 2004 Worrell applied to purchase a shotgun at a shop near Atlanta, Georgia. Though applying under his own name, he signified two false-hoods: that he'd never been indicted for a felony and that he'd never been committed to a psychiatric institution. The background check showed otherwise—and that the state of New York wanted him for jumping bail.

District attorneys in New York began to investigate Ham's assault case again. Though such evidence as the original 911 call were long since lost, the underwear Ms. Ham wore that night still remained in storage. It had been of little use in the 1970s, but now it provided crucial DNA evidence—proof that Worrell was Ms. Ham's rapist, as well as the assailant in some two dozen other cases.

In November 2005 Ms. Ham testified in court again, telling the story of that long-ago night, and how she'd lived with it ever since. This time the court quickly convicted Worrell. "I feel very, very vindicated," she told reporters at a news conference. "It's taken a long time."★

Is grace weak compared to evil? The answer seems to be yes. I could hit someone with a car and change their life forever, but courteously waving someone into my lane ahead of me probably isn't going to make that much of a difference in the long run. So what good is grace?

People pray every day for miracles: "Help me pass this test." "Help me get that job." "Help my boss not to notice." What they're really asking for, though, isn't a miracle, but magic. They want God to wave a wand over them, not involve them in the careful and protracted work of changing their hearts. Grace is far more than forgiveness—it is everything He does for us, from transforming us to just showing His love in an infinite variety of ways. And that's where grace comes in—not with a bang, but a balm.

## Reach out and touch someone

Frederick II (1194-1250) wasn't your ordinary Holy Roman Emperor. Endlessly curious, history records that he spoke nine languages and read seven. A patron of science and the arts, he reformed laws and economics, and questioned anything and everything. A religious skeptic, he denounced Christianity, Judaism, and Islam alike. People called him *stupor mundi*—the "wonder (or astonishment) of the world." He wrote scientific books on birds and falconry, was the first ruler to forbid doctors (who diagnosed diseases) from doubling as pharmacists (who sold drugs), and thanks to his regular wars with the papal states, Pope Gregory IX declared him the antichrist.

Yet today, Frederick II is perhaps most often remembered for a tragic experiment. Frederick wanted to discover people's original language, so he borrowed a number of newborn babies from their families. Foster mothers fed and bathed the infants, but were forbidden to speak to, hold, rock, cuddle, or otherwise interact with them. Every one of the children soon died without speaking a word. As the historian Salimbene wrote in 1248: "They could not live without petting."

Frederick's ghastly experiment inadvertently highlighted a central truth of humanity: Touch is essential to survival. We're born craving it, thrive on it, and die inside and out for the lack of it. Babies need touch to grow. Stroking their skin prompts their cells to divide faster and absorb more nutrients.

The sense of touch communicates affection, protection, and direction. No crimes are looked down upon more than distortions of it. Touch transmits assurance, patience, and relationship. It tells us that we're not alone, not forsaken, and can't be shaken. Touch is life. And touch has power to heal.

An August 1997 *Life* magazine article, "The Healing Power of Touch," by George Howe Colt, reported that more than 50 Touch Research Institute studies had shown massage to have positive effects on conditions from colic to hyperactivity to diabetes to migraines—in fact, on every malady TRI had studied so far. Massage, it seems, may help asthmatics breathe easier, improve autistic children's ability to concentrate, and relax burn victims about to undergo debridement, the painful procedure of removing damaged skin.

"When we say that somebody touches us emotionally, it means he or she has gone to the core of our being. Physical touch, too, is more than skin-deep. Skin is the human body's largest organ, containing millions of receptors—about 8,000 in a single fingertip—that send messages through nerve fibers to the spinal cord and then to the brain. A simple touch—a hand on a shoulder, an arm around a waist—can reduce the heart rate and lower blood pressure. Even people in deep comas may show improved heart rates when their hands are held. Positive, nurturing touch stimulates the release of endorphins, the body's natural pain suppressors. That may explain why a mother's hug can literally 'make it better' when a child skins his knee."

Describing the benefits of massage on a premature infant, the article noted, "With three massages a day for 10 days, he should be more alert, active and responsive than nonmassaged infants of his size and condition. He may have fewer episodes of apnea [a brief cessation of breathing]. . . . He should gain weight 47 percent faster."

Of course, the article notes, touch isn't the only thing that can stimulate endorphin production. So can cocaine—which is why touch deprivation may be one of the strongest contributors to addictive behaviors.

In the beginning, God spoke everything into existence in a creative explosion: light. Oceans. Trees. Grass. Mammoths. Dolphins. Watermelons. Sunflowers. Salamanders. Let there be light. Let there be land. Let the water teem with living creatures. Like, we might say, magic.

God spoke into existence all things but one: human beings. People weren't just declared into life. People were handcrafted. And that makes all the difference. That's grace. Grace doesn't look for a quick fix—it gets down and dirty.

"The Lord God formed the man from the dust of the ground and breathed into his nostrils the breath of life, and the man became a living being" (Gen. 2:7).

In all our intricate, intimate detail, God molded us by hand. Carefully, pleasure-takingly, God formed our hearts, knees, spines, and eyes. The Creator packed our minds with capacity—to love, to wonder, to feel, to know, to grow.

If grace doesn't usually work like magic (suddenly and abruptly), it's because that's not how God made us in the beginning. He sculpted us with care. Though violence is quick and selfish, grace is as subtle and delicate as our souls. There is no "cheap grace," for grace takes its time, and time is investment. Violence and magic is a declaration of independence—of noninvolvement—while true grace reminds us how much we need each other. Grace isn't the bursting of dynamite but the cracking of ice, the shedding of scorn, the weaving of wonder.

Christians have flinched at grace because guilt seems a greater—and quicker—motivator. As a result millions have rejected the church for its coating of condemnation. But true spirituality is based not on guilt, but on gratitude.

Social scientists classify religiosity under two basic labels: extrinsic and intrinsic. While many find religion as liberating, promoting health, stronger relationships, and happiness, it can also be detrimental and enslaving. Authoritarianism and literalism characterize the latter kind of religion. It transforms God's blessings into curses. Extrinsic religion is rigid and guilt-driven, focused on outward displays. Such religion sees everything as a means to an end and uses and abuses even people.

Intrinsic religion, on the other hand, has as its motivation gratitude, not guilt. This kind of religion thrives not on ritual but relationship. We serve God and seek to glorify Him because of what He has done for us, and our actions flow naturally from within. As Jesus said: "The good man brings good things out of the good stored up in his heart, and the evil man brings evil things out of the evil stored up in his heart. For out of the overflow of his heart his mouth speaks" (Luke 6:45).

I believe grace is more powerful than evil—we just don't see enough of it. And it operates differently. Violence works from the outside in, while grace flows from the inside out. And while violence shatters, grace revitalizes. Grace transforms everything about our lives and religious experience. It changes our motives from proving a point to demonstrating love. Worship focuses on praise, not proving yourself. The Sabbath goes from a day of self-centered asceticism to a day of service to others. Families flourish as people grow together.

A lot of people picture God like a man I know only as "Mr. Bubbles." During my senior class trip my classmates and I enjoyed a spirited time at the beach in St. Augustine, Florida, and topped off our day with some hearty helpings of pizza. When we stepped outside of the pizza parlor to continue on our way, however, we met trouble—trouble with a capital Bubble. We had parked our bus on the property of Mr. Bubbles' car wash, and Mr. Bubbles wasn't happy. In fact, he was so upset that we were infringing on his business, he wasn't going to let us leave.

While we watched in stunned bewilderment (and snapped pictures of ourselves in front of the vehicles Mr. Bubbles had parked to prevent our departure), our phlegmatic bus driver/class sponsor had a good talk with the angry businessman. Mr. Bubbles must have decided he'd vented enough, for suddenly we were free to go.

Is God ever like that, so upset at our sin that He's reluctant to forgive it? The Bible gives as clear a no as could ever be written. When we pray, Jesus tells us, "Before [you] call I will answer" (Isa. 65:24). When we sin, God's answer is even more astonishing, for before humanity fell, Jesus was ready to die. Revelation describes Jesus as "the Lamb slain from the foundation of the world" (Rev. 13:8, KJV).

## Purr

As I slowly awoke to a glorious day away from the office this morning, I heard a sound like a heralding trumpet piped through feline lips: "Brillig! Brillig! Brillig!" Then three scratches on the carpet like the hoofbeats of horses. Suddenly a cat leaped upon me and settled down, a sound like a rushing waterfall roaring from its chest. It was our family's tawny tomcat, and the sound of his purr always sounds to me like victory.

He was a scrap of nothing when some friends brought him to us, a bleary-eyed bundle of skin and something resembling fur. Rescued from the streets where neighborhood kids had mistreated him, he flourished in our house, gobbling up food and batting at toys and streams of water from the faucets with abandon. We named him Biscuit for his coloring. Still, even as he grew up, signs of his kittenhood deprivation remained. His fur was prickly like a camel hair coat. He bristled at our touch. And he never purred, only occasionally making a sound like a choked breath.

My sister Bronwen made "taming" Biscuit her goal. Finally she managed to hold him a few moments—cradled in tissue paper.

When he was about 7 years old, we noticed something different about Biscuit. His fur was no longer prickly—it was soft. We marveled and petted him, not just to feel his new fuzziness, but in joy.

One evening my mother stretched out on her back on the couch with a book, and Biscuit leaped onto her stomach. As she ran her fingers through his fur she heard the first stirrings of a new sensation. At almost 10 years of age, Biscuit had finally gotten his purr.

Yes, grace is a sticky subject. But in the long run it's the only thing that sticks.

---

*Adapted from "For '73 Rape Victim, DNA Revives Horror, Too," New York *Times,* Nov. 3, 2005.

# Wise as Serpents, Harmless as Doves

## CHAPTER 12

*"The fear of the Lord teaches a man wisdom, and humility comes before honor" (Prov. 15:33).*

Knuckles bloodied, the prince helped the slave to his feet. The slave stared at his taskmaster's body, crumpled in the desert sand.

"Are you all right?" the prince asked. His heart hammering, he tried to grasp what he'd just done. Though he lived in luxury, he could not forget his people the Hebrews, slaves to the country he'd been raised to rule. Surely God had put him in the palace to rescue them. The Egyptian overseer had beaten his slave just because he didn't like his attitude. Well, just what kind of attitude did he expect a slave to have?

"You're—you're Prince Moses!" the slave exclaimed. "My master—he's dead, isn't he?"

"Yes. Now run!"

Glancing back once more, the slave bolted toward his work crew. His friends wouldn't believe this.

Moses scanned the empty horizon as he dug into the sand. No eyes but the slave's had seen what he'd just done. Burying the body as deeply as possible, he took the long way back to the palace.

The next day he rushed to the sight of two men fighting—two Hebrews. "How can you hit your fellow Hebrew?" he demanded.

"What's it to you?" the man sneered. "What are you gonna do—kill me the way you did that Egyptian?"

His stomach twisting, Moses thought, *Everybody knows—and Pharaoh is going to kill me.* He hurled himself toward Midian. If God wanted to rescue the Hebrews, He'd just have to find another guy. Now Moses had some lambs to herd.

## Jerusalem

*Something big's going down tonight—I can feel it,* Peter thought, squirming to get comfortable as he stretched out on the stony ground. *Whatever happens, I'm . . . ready . . . for . . . action . . .*

"Are you still sleeping?" His Master's voice cut through the fog. "Rise—let's go! Here comes My betrayer!"

*Betrayer? Now?* Peter scrambled to his feet. Torches lit up a horde of men with swords and clubs. *Judas. So that's where he's been—*

The mob pushed and shoved. Seizing Jesus, they began to bind His wrists behind Him.

Instantly Peter grabbed the sword at his side. This was the moment he'd lived for, the day the rebellion would begin. Jesus had proclaimed His kingship only a few days before. The people were ready to join His army. Peter had long pictured himself leading the charge. He slashed the air toward the nearest available target—Malchus, servant of the high priest. The sword sliced through the man's ear.

The crowd froze as Jesus reached out and healed Malchus, mindless of the men working to bind Him. Then He turned to Peter. "Put your sword away," He said, "for all who draw the sword will die by it. Don't you know I could pray to My Father, and He could send thousands of angels to help Me? But then how would Scripture be fulfilled?"

Like frightened sheep, Peter and the other disciples scattered. If Jesus wanted to go down in flames, He didn't need their help.

## Wise as serpents, harmless as doves

When the Jews pictured their Messiah, they expected an almighty king who would conquer their earthly enemies. Few thought of the lambs they offered as sacrifice.

As their Master lay in a tomb, the disciples remembered back over the past three years. Had Jesus not proclaimed a new kingdom? Had He not trained them for action? This couldn't be the end—could it?

Peter remembered the day Jesus commissioned the twelve as His disciples. He sent them out on a mission for His kingdom, but they were to be no ordinary soldiers. They were never to use force to accomplish their goals. Instead, with the Holy Spirit as their ally, they were to change the world one person at a time through the power of love.

"When he saw the crowds, he had compassion on them, because they were harassed and helpless, like sheep without a shepherd. Then he said to his disciples, 'The harvest is plentiful, but the workers are few'" (Matt. 9:36, 37).

"Preach this message: 'The kingdom of heaven is near,'" Jesus instructed the twelve. "Heal the sick, raise the dead, cleanse those who have leprosy, drive out demons" (Matt. 10:7, 8).

The mission would not be easy. It would meet stiff resistance. Hated and persecuted, His followers would find themselves hauled before governors and kings. Their message would divide families and stir up trouble. "I'm sending you out like sheep among wolves," Jesus said.

His mission instructions:

▶ *Heal the sick, raise the dead, restore the outcast, drive out demons.* Everything their Master had done, the disciples were authorized to do as His representatives.

▶ *"Freely you have received, freely give"* (verse 8). The gospel is not for sale. Though "the worker is worth his keep" (verse 10), the gospel has no place for greed. The disciples were not to worry about money, clothes, or possessions.

▶ *Wherever you go, find a worthy person to stay with.* If some place does not welcome you, shake the dust off your feet when you leave the town.

▶ *Be as shrewd as snakes and innocent as doves.* Jesus' workers were to be discerning, alert, clever, and wise. At the same time, they must be as untainted and unaffected by the world as doves.

▶ *Be on your guard.* The mission was dangerous, but Jesus would be with them.

▶ *Don't worry about what to say or how to say it.* When arrested and summoned before authorities for Jesus' sake, His representatives could trust Him completely even if their mission brought them into danger, because the Holy Spirit would speak through them.

▶ *What I told you privately, you should proclaim in public.* His teachings weren't just for a select few—they were for the whole world. While He had nurtured only a few people in His short time on earth, His followers would multiply His influence a millionfold.

▶*Don't fear those who kill the body but cannot kill the soul.* God's watching over you.

After Jesus' death and resurrection His disciples at last understood. Their mission wasn't to take life—it was to give it. They were not to fight evil with force, but to overcome it with good. To kill for God would be easy. The real challenge was to live and die for Him. With the Holy Spirit working for them, they'd turn the world upside down.

Our role in the war between good and evil is to show God's love. From AIDS victims to the homeless, to the mentally ill, to the girl sitting behind you in science class, people are dying for lack of love.

"The King will reply, 'I tell you the truth, whatever you did for one of the least of these brothers of mine, you did for me'" (Matt. 25:40).

Jesus won the war at the cross. The universe at last understood the true difference between good and evil, and saw the true character of God. And soon we'll join them in celebration at the sea of glass, singing the song of Moses and the Lamb (Rev. 15:3).

# Overcome Evil With Good

## CHAPTER 13

*"Let love be genuine; hate what is evil, hold fast to what is good; love one another with mutual affection; outdo one another in showing honor. Do not lag in zeal, be ardent in spirit, serve the Lord. Rejoice in hope, be patient in suffering, persevere in prayer. Contribute to the needs of the saints; extend hospitality to strangers. Bless those who persecute you; bless and do not curse them" (Rom. 12:9-14, NRSV).*

*A*s Rwanda roiled with relentless slaughter, Carl Wilkens was the only American left in the country.

Two main ethnic groups inhabit Rwanda: Hutus and Tutsis. About 15 percent of the country's population are Tutsis, primarily cattle herders. The majority are Hutu, mostly peasant farmers. When the Belgian government took over Rwanda as a colony, they pitted the two groups against each other, pointing out their supposed differences and giving Tutsis more political power. When Rwanda gained independence in the 1960s, Hutus assumed control and took revenge, and many Tutsis fled.

By 1994 Wilkens; his wife, Teresa; and their three small children had lived in Rwanda together for four years. Serving as the country director for the Adventist Development and Relief Agency, he found the country a peaceful, beautiful place, just as it had been when he'd previously served there during the early

1980s. When civil war broke out in part of the country shortly after Wilkens' arrival in 1990, with exiled Tutsis demanding an end to Hutu domination, he went from building schools and health centers to serving refugees fleeing the crisis.

In early 1994 the civil war looked headed to a peaceful resolution, with Hutus and Tutsis agreeing to share power—but Wilkens sensed trouble brewing. He heard rumors of pickup trucks loaded with machetes appearing throughout the country. In February he faxed church headquarters with an urgent message: the country was sitting on a "keg of dynamite." Church leaders began drawing up plans to evacuate all missionaries.

Wilkens' parents were visiting Carl at their home in Kigali, the capital, lending a hand with finances and other detail work. Working with them at his office the night of Wednesday, April 6, Wilkens heard explosions in the distance. "Boy," his father said, "that was no grenade."

A missile had shot down the plane of Rwandan president Habyarimana, a Hutu. The Tutsis accused militant Hutus of causing the crash in order to turn people against Tutsis and at the same time seize power. But Hutu leaders blamed it on Tutsis—and called for the murder of all Tutsis in Rwanda. Soldiers and militia members went door to door, calling Hutus to "come out and start your work. The job has begun." The people must not think of their victims as their friends and neighbors—they were killing inyenzi, "cockroaches," pests who deserved to die.

*"Rejoice with those who rejoice, weep with those who weep"* (verse 15, NRSV).

Within hours the violence surrounded Wilkens' mission compound home, located in what became one of the deadliest parts of the city. Carl and Teresa did their best to keep their children's attention focus elsewhere with improvised games, telling them to move about only when they didn't hear gunfire.

Church officials ordered Wilkens out of the country. He wrestled with what to do. While he wanted his family safe, he couldn't just leave his Tutsi friends to die. His parents urged him to leave. Carl's father, a man with a long career in the church, told him that if staying behind didn't end his life, his noncompliance could terminate his church career.

Still, Teresa understood how her husband felt. They prayed together again and again about his decision to stay, and he asked, "Does this still seem right?"

Teresa looked at her husband of 13 years—her high school sweetheart, the father of her children. "Yes, it does."

Laura Lane, an officer at the American embassy in Kigali as the genocide began, barely slept those first few days, contacting every American to help them get out. Lane remembers Wilkens well, having been in touch with him since he came to Rwanda in 1990. "He could be hardheaded because he thinks things should be done a certain way. But he had such a strength of purpose—you were amazed by the conviction, whether or not you agreed with him. I remember thinking I admired him, but he frustrated me to no end. I was responsible for getting all the Americans out of harm's way, but having to battle with someone who had to have things done a certain way."

Carl called Lane on the radio. "I'm sending my family," he said.

A pause. "Wait," Laura said. "What do you mean you're sending your family?"

"Well, Laura, I'm not leaving."

"No, you don't understand," she protested. "Other times there were options. There's no option this time. You have to come out with them."

"Laura," he replied, "as a private citizen, I think I can make that choice."

They argued further, until Laura said, "You need to write down that you've refused the help of the U.S. government to evacuate."

Pulling out a piece of his children's school notebook paper, Carl carefully composed a note. He folded it up and handed it to Teresa.

On Sunday Carl watched as his wife, children, and parents pulled away in a caravan of vehicles, each marked with a white T-shirt. "It just seemed the right thing to do," he told *New York Times* columnist Nicholas Kristof. "I could take my blue passport and go, and moments later my housegirl and night watchman, both identifiable Tutsis, were going to be butchered." Instead, he walked back through his gate and locked it, then knelt on the floor of his house with his Tutsi servants, praying for his family's safety. He felt powerless and empty.

*"Live in harmony with one another; do not be haughty, but associate with the lowly; do not claim to be wiser than you are"* (verse 16, NRSV).

"[Before the genocide Hutus and Tutsis] worked together, worshipped together, married together, drank beer together," Wilkens reflected in a 2003 interview. "They did everything together. . . . [Yet] those who were orchestrating [mass murder] knew exactly what buttons to push to enflame this." Soon violence swept the streets, the villages, the farmlands.

How did so many "ordinary" people become vicious killers? Through the first trick of every propagandist: *fear.* Rumors and radio broadcasts highlighted the alleged dangers and evils Tutsis posed to Rwanda, playing on Hutus' imaginations. Motivated by fear and resentment for social slights real and imagined, thousands of "normal" Rwandans murdered friends, customers, children. Some 800,000 perished in all, an average of 10,000 a day.

To have any effect against such fear, one would have to be fearless.

## Things They Never Taught Me

The American embassy closed and nearly all foreigners left. The leaders of the violence proclaimed that the world had turned its back on the Tutsis, so Hutus were free to kill them. "God doesn't want them," they claimed. "Nobody wants them."

*"Do not repay anyone evil for evil, but take thought for what is noble in the sight of all"* (verse 17, NRSV).

Wilkens waited in his house for three weeks as chaos reigned outside. Recognizing that he might never make it out alive, he began making audiotapes for Teresa:

"Whew, I guess I didn't talk much about Sunday's mean gun battle. Man, I just stayed on a mattress in the hallway, holding my Bible on my chest . . ."

"[gunfire] Brought the animals all inside. The monkey is tied up to the sink in our bathroom. He doesn't like this very well."

Hutus in the neighborhood knew Carl was hiding Tutsis in his house. Their threats were far from idle: "Next time your White man comes out, we're going to kill him." But neighbors defended him: "Don't kill them—they are missionaries. . . . These people aren't a part of this. Their kids play with our kids, and when we're sick, they take us to the hospital."

Carl kept in touch with the outside world through phone calls and radio. When militia came by, he bribed them with whatever he could give away—dishes, a watch. Finally, after three weeks, a curfew lifted, and he could venture outside. He decided to travel with a Rwandan pastor to check on ADRA's offices and warehouses.

*"If it is possible, so far as it depends on you, live peaceably with all"* (verse 18, NRSV).

Kigali felt like a ghost town. Horses roamed freely, freed from their stalls at the Belgian country club. Most of the bodies had been cleared from the streets, but barriers and roadblocks were everywhere, overseen by drunken men on couches waving bloody machetes, old shotguns cradled across their laps. Everything had been looted, especially the warehouses.

Wilkens began traveling daily. He made it his mission to take food, water, and medical supplies to the area orphanages and to assist anyone he could. Frequently he ferried people to the Red Cross hospital for treatment. And he talked with anyone and everyone who could aid him to help others. "Whenever you're in nasty situations, you're looking for an ally, and sometimes you find allies where you would never expect," Wilkens remembers. One such ally was a colonel in Kigali, a man who would later be sentenced for crimes against humanity. One day the colonel told militia members not to hassle Wilkens, and he began to get through town without being stopped constantly.

The thought of leaving each morning would make Wilkens' stomach knot, and he prayed for protection and guidance. He felt God telling him, *OK, you have the peace—go out now.*

Carl risked his life every moment outside his house, dodging bullets, rockets, and rocks as he traveled. He joined up with U.N. worker Alex Gregory, delivering food to United Nations and Red Cross safe havens sheltering thousands of Tutsis. Dozens of times men surrounded their vehicles, shaking them, each one running a finger across his own throat to let them know they could be the next to die. Gregory worried that Carl was getting too bold, too obsessed, forgetting that he would do no good if he were dead.

One day a bullet blew out the back window and passed through the driver's headrest of his Toyota Corolla as Wilkens crept around outside to unlock the passenger's side of the vehicle. A 44-gallon drum of water, destined for an orphanage, had fallen off the dump truck he was following. He'd intended to put the drum in his own truck, and didn't know why he felt compelled to un-lock the passenger door—until he found himself having to climb back in his truck through that door, sliding into the bulleted driver's seat, and taking off.

"There were times of real hopelessness," Carl reported later. "I basically had to say to myself, 'There's nothing I can do about that.' I could spend a lot of time in anger about why other people weren't making a difference, weren't doing it, but that wasn't going to stop anything."

Wilkens wondered how far he should go to save lives. Was it possible to compromise too much in dealing with killers?

And then there was the Gisimba orphanage.

*"Beloved, never avenge yourselves, but leave room for the wrath of God; for it is writ-ten, 'Vengeance is mine, I will repay, says the Lord'"* (verse 19, NSRV),

The colonel in Kigali had told Wilkens about the Gisimba orphanage, located in one of the bloodiest parts of the city, overrun by some of the most vicious killers. Adults and children were being murdered and dying of starvation and dysentery.

One day, traveling with a Rwandan colleague, Carl arrived to drop off a load of water. One of the orphanage director's younger brothers ran out to meet him. "Where's your brother?" Wilkens asked.

The director had gone to try to find help and food. "They came last night," the brother said. "They killed some people. They said they're coming back to finish us all off today."

A Mercedes station wagon sped up to them. As the driver got out of the car, suddenly about 50 camouflage-clad, machine gun-toting militia members sur-rounded them.

Wilkens wrestled with what to do. Finally he decided he should go for aid. "I'll come back," he promised the director's brother. "I can get help." The brother urged him not to go, and Wilkens feared he was leaving the orphanage to its grisly fate—that he'd be stopped and shot at the next barrier. Still, he and his Rwandan partner headed to the nearby police camp to look for the man in charge. They'd met him before—before the violence.

The man wished he could help, but he didn't have anybody he could send. "Maybe I'll try the army," Wilkens said. He called the military camp's phone, but no one answered.

Next Carl headed to headquarters to look for the colonel. The secretary told him the officer had left for the day. "But you won't believe it—the prime minister's here."

"So what's that mean?" Wilkens wondered aloud. When it came to the genocide, the prime minister was one of the guiltiest men in the country. Coordinating the violence, he'd urged death on his fellow citizens. What good could possibly come out of speaking with him? And yet—what other option was there? He might as well, since he was here . . .

"Just go out in the hallway," the secretary said. "He's in the next office. When he comes out, ask him."

Wilkens stepped into the hall. Soon the door opened. Everyone snapped to attention at the sight of the prime minister and his aides. Carl put out his hand.

"Mr. Prime Minister, I'm Carl Wilkins, the director of ADRA."

The prime minister stopped and looked at the audacious aid worker—then took his hand and shook it. "Yes, I've heard about you and your work. How is it?"

"Well, honestly, sir, it's not very good right now. The orphans at

Gisimba are surrounded, and I think there's going to be a massacre, if there hasn't been already."

The prime minister spoke with his men for a moment, then turned back to Wilkens. "We're aware of the situation, and those orphans are going to be safe. I'll see to it."

Well—now what? And what did the prime minister mean? But Wilkens realized he'd done all he could. It was getting late—and louder outside. He chose to go home—and trust. A few days later he found the orphans alive, transported to a safer part of town.

*"No, 'if your enemies are hungry, feed them; if they are thirsty, give them something to drink; for by doing this you will heap burning coals on their heads' "* (verse 20, NRSV).

## The power of presence, the power of choice

People have far more power for good and for evil than they realize, Wilkens says. "We all think there's a line we would never cross, and the people in Rwanda all thought the same thing," he explains. "If you would have said to them three months earlier, 'Even with a baby tied on your back, you'd be hacking your neighbor to death,' they would have said, 'That's ridiculous. You're insane.' The common moral compass of a society is a lot more fragile than any of us would ever want to know."

When Wilkens stayed behind in Rwanda, he had no specific intent other than to protect his Tutsi employees, and to make what difference he could by simply being there. "I had no plan but to be there," he explains. "There is a power of presence. African people understand that. They will come and maybe sit there for an hour and never say a word. Maybe just sit out on the porch."

There's power in standing up, of not being afraid to stand out. There's power in taking care of the small things, from picking up litter to defending someone who's criticized. And there's power in realizing you have a choice. Today Wilkens tells audiences, "Just because somebody tells you that you don't have a choice, you don't have to give them that power. People can limit our choices, but nobody can take our choices away, except us."

One person, he reminds us, can make a difference.

*"Do not be overcome by evil, but overcome evil with good"* (verse 12:21, NRSV).

# A Mirror to Evil

## CHAPTER 14

*"He [the Spirit of the Lord] has sent me to proclaim freedom for the prisoners and recovery of sight for the blind, to release the oppressed."—Jesus (Luke 4:18).*

*"You have heard that it was said, 'Eye for eye, and tooth for tooth.' But I tell you, Do not resist an evil person. If someone strikes you on the right cheek, turn to him the other also."—Jesus (Matt. 5:38, 39).*

*"And now I will show you the more excellent way."—Paul (1 Cor. 12:31).*

*"Love never fails."—Paul (1 Cor. 13:8).*

There's nothing more dangerous to oppressors than an idea. Which is why the narrow-minded fear ideas more than any weapon, for free minds have toppled a thousand despotic houses of cards.

Englishman Peter Benenson's idea seemed ludicrous. Early critics called it "one of the larger lunacies of our time." Yet it grew to change the lives of countless suffering people.

A newspaper report about two Portugese students sparked it. In 1960 Benenson read about two young men sentenced to seven years in prison—for the high crime of raising their glasses and toasting freedom. At the time dictator

Salazar held Portugal in a tight grip, controlling the press and crushing dissent.

Benenson wondered how he could help the students escape such an unjust fate. Then again, how could someone save *any* of the countless people imprisoned just because they disagreed with their government or practiced an unapproved religion? A vigilante army of would-be Rambos cracking heads—and inspiring more bloodshed and harsher persecution? Merely prayer? Prayer was invaluable, but never as an excuse for inaction.

As a citizen of another country, Benenson's concern appeared powerless. But he knew something the world's tyrants and stubborn governments didn't: *right makes might, and no weapon in that fight is more powerful than love.* Love lifts up. Love never gives up. Love spurs the righteous and shames the wicked. Love never fails.

His solution was simple: Write a letter. Not just one letter, of course, but a steady stream of them from people around the world, each asking the Salazar regime to set their prisoners of conscience free. Such letters would let dictators know that their actions were not hidden, their oppressed citizens not invisible. That the world saw their actions and that people cared and would not give up until the oppressed were free.

Benenson enlisted two well-connected friends, the renowned Quaker Eric Baker and the internationally respected lawyer Louis Blom-Cooper, and an idea came to life: "Appeal for Amnesty 1961." They would open the world's eyes on behalf of anyone imprisoned solely for their political or religious views.

The 1961 campaign pinpointed eight "forgotten prisoners," including Ashton Jones, a 65-year-old pastor who had been repeatedly jailed and beaten in Texas and Louisiana for advocating civil rights for Blacks; the archbishop of Prague, imprisoned for his opposition to Czechoslovakia's Communist government; Patrick Duncan, a White South African who opposed his country's racist policy of apartheid; and Dr. Agostino Neto, who would later become independent Angola's first president.

The idea caught fire around the world. People formed groups and "adopted" specific prisoners, contacting and encouraging prisoners' families while bombarding oppressive governments with letters demanding freedom. They also wrote letters to the prisoners themselves, hoping that they would learn that no matter how invisible and discarded they felt, they were really not alone.

Soon Benenson and his group started seeing results—and what started as a crazy idea became the human rights organization Amnesty International, an agency dedicated to nonviolent advocacy, political impartiality, and the principle that no one, anywhere, should be punished for thinking different. Their logo, a candle surrounded by barbed wire, reflects the old saying "Better to light a candle than to curse the darkness."

A former prisoner of conscience in the Dominican Republic shared his story:

"When the first 200 letters came, the guards gave me back my clothes. Then the next 200 letters came, and the prison director came to see me. When the next pile of letters arrived, the director got in touch with his superior. The letters kept coming and coming; 3,000 of them. The president was informed. The letters still kept arriving, and the president called the prison and told them to let me go."

**A mirror to evil**

The frightening fact is that every one of us holds as much potential for great evil as great good.

I'll never forget a picture I saw of two Black men hanging in a tree, while a crowd of Whites stood around looking almost blasé.

They were not random hoodlums—they were the cream of "polite society," dressed in their Sunday best: an old women in a fur coat, men in white shirts and ties and derby hats, a young woman in a paisley dress. Like Sodom's marauding mob, the crowd had people of all ages, and each gave their tacit support to oppression, violence, and murder—then went back to church on Sunday, clicking their tongues. The dirty but not so little secret was that the early twentieth century saw an average of 60 lynchings a year in America. People even sold postcards of the sickening scenes.

In 1963 the American civil rights movement seemed at a standstill. The Montgomery, Alabama, bus boycott was eight years behind them. In 1960 students across the South, inspired by Martin Luther King's book on nonviolence, *Stride Toward Freedom,* had staged successful sit-ins at segregated lunch counters. The students sat still, refusing to react with rudeness or violence while storeowners and onlookers taunted, shoved, or burned their skin with cigarettes. Their nonviolent resistance had stirred consciences, and soon restaurants, public parks, swimming pools, libraries, and beaches opened to all.

But now critics suggested that King and his colleagues stop agitating while they were ahead. They'd accomplished so much—why keep stirring things up? For King, though, there was only one way for the civil rights movement to go: forward. He wanted not just to respond to a crisis, but to see just how far nonviolence could go in shaping hearts and minds.

King wanted to hold up a mirror to the evil in people's hearts, so that they could finally see for themselves the reality of their attitudes. The words of

Gandhi, who won independence for India through nonviolent action, had long inspired him: "Through our pain we will make them see their injustice." It was the toughest kind of love there is.

Finally King decided to go to Birmingham, Alabama, where racist violence shook the community. His group prepared to launch Project C, for Confrontation. But even the Black community was far from sure about the approach. The local government had issued an injunction that King could not lead a march. And a group of eight White Alabaman pastors had written him an open letter telling him to chill. Yet King chose to march anyway, and landed in the Birmingham jail. Locked inside, he wrote a reply to the White pastors in the margins of a newspaper.

### "Our very bodies"

Point by point he responded to the ministers. "In any nonviolent campaign there are four basic steps: collection of the facts to determine whether injustices exist; negotiation; self-purification; and direct action. We have gone through all these steps in Birmingham. There can be no gainsaying the fact that racial injustice engulfs this community. Birmingham is probably the most thoroughly segregated city in the United States. Its ugly record of brutality is widely known. . . . There have been more unsolved bombings of Negro homes and churches in Birmingham than in any other city in the nation. These are the hard, brutal facts of the case. . . . Negro leaders sought to negotiate with the city fathers. But the latter consistently refused to engage in good-faith negotiation. . . .

"As in so many past experiences, our hopes bad been blasted, and the shadow of deep disappointment settled upon us. We had no alternative except to prepare for direct action, whereby we would present our very bodies as a means of laying our case before the conscience of the local and the national community. Mindful of the difficulties involved, we decided to undertake a process of self-purification. We began a series of workshops on nonviolence, and we repeatedly asked ourselves, 'Are you able to accept blows without retaliation?' 'Are you able to endure the ordeal of jail?' . . .

"You may well ask: 'Why direct action? Why sit-ins, marches, and so forth? Isn't negotiation a better path?' You are quite right in calling for negotiations. Indeed, this is the very purpose of direct action. Nonviolent direct actions seek to create such a crisis and foster such a tension that a community which has constantly refused to negotiate is forced to confront the issue. It seeks so to dramatize the issue that it can no longer be ignored. My citing the creation of tension as part of the work of the nonviolent-resister may sound rather shocking. But I must confess that I am not afraid of the word 'tension.' I have earnestly opposed violent tension, but there is a type of constructive, nonviolent tension which is necessary for growth. . . . We see the need for nonviolent gadflies to create the kind of tension in society that will help men rise from the dark depths of prejudice and racism to the majestic heights of understanding and brotherhood.

"The purpose of our direct-action program is to create a situation so crisis-packed that it will inevitably open the door to negotiation. I therefore concur with you in your call for negotiation. Too long has our beloved Southland been bogged down in a tragic effort to live in monologue rather than dialogue."

Birmingham put King behind bars, but footage of their police unleashing dogs and fire hoses on men, women, and children shocked Americans out of their complacence. The moral victory was won, and a year later America's Congress passed the Civil Rights Act.

## "Something had gone out of our lives forever"

Love never forces its way. Yet it has a powerful, seductive enemy, a false god that's inspired even the most God-fearing, Jesus-loving people to betray all they stand for: war.

In 1984 screenwriter *(The Polar Express, Apollo 13)* William Broyles, Jr., a Vietnam veteran, authored an essay for *Esquire* magazine titled "Why Men Love War." "That's why," he wrote, "when we returned from Vietnam, we moped around, listless, not interested in anything or anyone. Something had gone out of our lives forever, and our behavior on returning was inexplicable except as the behavior of men who had lost a great—perhaps the great—love of their lives, and had no way to tell anyone about it."

Pulitzer prize-winning journalist Chris Hedges saw war up close throughout the 1980s and 1990s. *In War Is a Force That Gives Us Meaning* he recalls, "I have been in ambushes on desolate stretches of Central American roads, shot at in the marshes of southern Iraq, imprisoned in the Sudan, beaten by Saudi military police, deported from Libya and Iran, captured and held for a week by the Iraqi Republican Guard during the Shiite rebellion following the Gulf War, strafed by Russian Mig-21s in Bosnia, fired upon by Serb snipers, and shelled for days in Sarajevo with deafening rounds of heavy artillery that threw out thousands of deadly bits of iron fragments. I have seen too much of violent death. I have tasted too much of my own fear. I have painful memories that lie buried and untouched most of the time. It is never easy when they surface" (Chris Hedges,

*War Is a Force That Gives Us Meaning* [New York: Public Affairs, 2002], pp. 2, 3).

His years of war-chasing helped him understand its powerful allure. Hedges describes war's "enduring attraction": "Even with its destruction and carnage it can give us what we long for in life. It can give us purpose, meaning, a reason for living. Only when we are in the midst of conflict does the shallowness and vapidness of much of our lives become apparent. . . . War is an enticing elixir. It gives us resolve, a cause. It allows us to be noble" (*ibid.,* p. 3).

For all that love brings—passion, a purpose to life, unity—war gives a super-charged counterfeit. Openness becomes exclusion. Myths become history. Writes Hedges, "War makes the world understandable. . . . It suspends thought, especially self-critical thought. All bow before the supreme effort. We are one. Most of us willingly accept war as long as we can fold it into a belief system that paints the ensuing suffering as necessary for a higher good, for human beings seek not only happiness but also meaning. And tragically war is sometimes the most powerful way in human society to achieve meaning.

"But war is a god, as the ancient Greeks and Romans knew, and its worship demands human sacrifice. We urge young men to war, making the slaughter they are asked to carry out a rite of passage. And this rite has changed little over the centuries, centuries in which there has almost continuously been a war raging somewhere on the planet. The historian Will Durant calculated that there have only been twenty-nine years in all of human history during which a war was not under way somewhere" (*ibid.,* p. 10).

For the soldier caught up in it, war offers as close to the Godlike power promised by Eden's serpent as is usually humanly possible. War destroys love by imitating it, yet worshipping only power.

## Sanctity

Hedges slept restlessly in war zones, his dreams full of violence and loss. Yet in the homes of couples in love he slept soundly. Their love shielded them from the lies of war. "Love, when it is deep and sustained by two individuals, includes self-giving—often self-sacrifice—as well as desire. For the covenant of love is such that it recognizes both the fragility and the sanctity of the individual. It recognizes itself in the other. It alone can save us" (*ibid.,* pp., 160, 161).

As the classic movie satire *Dr. Strangelove* (famous for the line "You can't fight in here! This is the War Room!") illustrates, humanity has a "strange love" for death and destruction. We've had it ever since we fell for the serpent's false promise of cheating death. The only antidote is self-sacrificial love.

In *Which Jesus?: Choosing Between Love and Power,* Tony Campolo writes of the choice between love and power. God has given up some of His power that we may have freedom. Jesus refused to display His power for the power-hungry religious leaders. And Campolo discusses the incredible power of love, too often left untried. History has shown again and again that only love can truly conquer the darkest evil.

Campolo tells the story of Metropolitan Kyril, leader of the Orthodox Church in Bulgaria during World War II. Thanks to such leadership as his, no Bulgarian Jews perished in Nazi death camps, despite the country's alliance with Nazi Germany.

When the Nazis came for Bulgaria's Jews, shoving them into boxcars at the Sophia, Bulgaria, train station, Kyril stepped in. "As the panic-stricken Jews, many sobbing hysterically, awaited their fate, a strange image appeared out of the drizzly, misty night. It was Metropolitan Kyril. He was a tall man to start with, but the miter

106

an Orthodox prelate wears on his head made him look like a giant. His flowing white beard hung down over his black robe, and it is said that his gait was such that the couple of hundred men who followed him had to hustle hard to keep up with him.

"As he approached the entrance of the barbed-wire enclosure, the SS guards raised their machine guns and told him, 'Father, you cannot go in there!' Metropolitan Kyril defiantly laughed at them, brushed aside the guns, and went into the midst of the Jewish prisoners. The apparently doomed Jews gathered around him, wondering what a leader of the Christian community would have to say to them at this desperate time. With arms upraised, Metropolitan Kyril recited one verse of Scripture from the book of Ruth. He helped to change the destiny of a nation as he shouted, 'Whithersoever you go, I will go—your people will be my people! Your God will be my God!'

"With these words, the frightened Jews were suddenly turned into an emboldened mob. They cheered their Christian friend. The Christians on the outside of the barbed wire enclosures cheered with them, and they became one in the Spirit. Responding to the noise at the train station, the townspeople came out of their houses and joined the crowd.

"The SS troops, surveying the scene, decided that discretion was the better part of valor. They boarded the train without their captives and left the town. What further evidence do we need to make the case that God's love can provide the motivation for history-changing action?" (*Which Jesus: Choosing Between Love and Power,* pp. 42, 43).

Cursing darkness is easy. Lighting a candle, showing and leading the way, takes courage, faith, hope, and love. But it's the only way forward, along the path Jesus blazed for us.

# It's the End of the World as We Know It

## CHAPTER 15

*"Immediately after the distress of those days*
  *'the sun will be darkened,*
  *and the moon will not give its light;*
  *the stars will fall from the sky,*
  *and the heavenly bodies will be shaken.'*
*At that time the sign of the Son of Man will appear in the sky,*
*and all the nations of the earth will mourn. They will see the*
*Son of Man coming on the clouds of the sky, with power and*
*great glory."*—Jesus (Matt. 24:29, 30).

If the Bible contained only the parts people normally read, it would be pretty short. Sometimes our Bible knowledge seems a bit like this:

God creates. Snake debates. Cain kills. Noah builds. Rain galore. Tower no more. Abe waits. Sodom bakes. Isaac's saved. Joseph slaves. Hebrews flee. Red Sea. Jericho. Dave and Go. Twenty-third psalm. Gilead balm. Fiery furnace. Prophets earnest. Lions' den. Wise men. Water into wine. Thousands dine. Jesus wept. Lame leapt. Calvary's tree. Victory. Galatian's law. John saw. Come again. Amen.

The truth, though, is that Scripture has a whole lot more than usually gets mentioned. In the sea of pages between Noah's ark and the beast's mark, we find the compelling picture of a God whose patience is beyond our understanding.

Judges, Kings, Jeremiah, Hosea—all demonstrate God's patience with people hell-bent on living life their own way. The book of Psalms shows God listening to the most desperate of prayers—even selfish ones. The Gospels tell us that after everything we've put God through He still wants—yea, longs for—us.

In *What the Bible Says About the End-time* (Review and Herald Publishing, 1994) Jon Paulien outlines the Bible's varying scenarios of how God will restore the world to perfection. To Abraham, God gave a threefold promise: descendants, blessings, and land. At Mount Sinai, God told the Israelites—the blessed descendants—that an angel would go ahead of them and drive their enemies from the Promised Land (Ex. 23:20-23). The Israelites messed up at Sinai, so in Deuteronomy 28 the Lord presented a gradual and conditional promise of complete restoration. God gave them two choices—

Choice One: Obey God and get His blessing.

Benefits: You'll be the greatest nation in the world—the top of the heap.

You'll prosper with healthy crops and bouncing babies.

Enemies will find it impossible to hurt you. The whole world will fear you because they know God is with you.

You'll be ridiculously successful in all that you do.

You'll even have great weather.

Cons: Um . . . um, you may need to add a few rooms to your house. And if you're a doctor, business might be a little slow.

Of course, there was also the ever-popular . . .

Choice Two: Do your own thing and go chasing after false, manipulative gods.

Benefits: If you're a doctor, you'll probably be quite busy . . . not that anyone can afford to pay you much.

Cons: Disaster and panic.

Pestilence.

Drought.

Disease.

Poverty.

Enemies will crush you.

You'll go into exile far from home.

You'll even be unlucky in love.

Did somebody mention cannibalism?

Well, you can't argue with a deal like that—follow God and get blessed out of your sandals, or leave His protection and reap the inevitable consequences of trying to live without His providence and protection. Unfortunately, as you might have figured out by now, the Israelites chose . . . Choice Two.

But even then God didn't write them off. He sent prophet after prophet to encourage, warn, and beg His people to give their hearts to Him. The book of Ezekiel shows God's fresh plans for a people He had to exile after centuries of wickedness, a plan marked by a final decisive battle. God would restore their hearts (Eze. 36:26, 27), their land (verse 28), and their nation. The Lord would defeat their enemies (Eze. 38; 39). A glorious new Temple was to be built and paradise restored.

Alas, even that plan fell through, as God's people traded carving idols out of wood and stone for making idols out of His commandments. Even then not much had changed—they still thought that they could succeed without a Savior, that they had something in themselves good enough not to need His help. That rituals could take the place of relationship.

Throughout history God has longed to bring us back to Him. And all along Satan has sought to prevent that by employing a pattern of deception, spreading lies about God's character, His law, the nature of death—anything to distract us from the truth.

**Hype and glory**

I sat down on the cold gymnasium bleachers next to my yawning classmates at the Christian academy I attended. It was 7:45 a.m. Class would begin in 15 minutes, but first we'd start our day with worship. The academy principal strode up to the front to give us the morning's message—a story he'd just recently heard.

"Two college students were driving along together on a trip," he began. "They were talking about world events when they saw a man out hitchhiking. Although they'd never picked up a hitchhiker before, for some reason they pulled over and let him in. He was a nicely dressed man, and he soon joined them in conversation. The two college guys started wondering how much longer the world would last—would Jesus come in the next 10 years? maybe even the next five?

"The hitchhiker spoke up from the back seat. 'Young men,' he said, 'Jesus is coming a lot sooner than you think.'

"'Why do you think so?' the college student riding shotgun asked. He turned around to look at the hitchhiker—but the hitchhiker was gone!"

I've forgotten the rest of the principal's morning message, but I do remember myself groaning (inside, not out loud). Hadn't he ever heard of the term *urban legend?* You know, those stories that go around that people swear are true, that they happened to a "friend of a friend," such as the woman who brought what she thought was a dog home from vacation, which turned out to be a rat, or the hook-handed serial killer? I was tempted to send him anonymously my family's copy of *The Vanishing Hitchhiker: American Urban Legends and Their Meanings,* a book that examined the appeal and phenomenon of such modern folk tales. Tales of prophetic passengers had been around since at least the day when someone found gloop oozing out of the ground and said, "Hey, I bet people could power their own personal trains with this—and they wouldn't even need rails."

"Let's pray," the principal said that day years ago. I closed my eyes as the principal began. "Dear God, thank You for promising to come soon. . . . And thank You, Jesus. that we live in a country where we have freedom, that we don't live in a country where secret police conduct sudden searches. . . . Amen. Have a great day, students, and oh, by the way—there will be a locker check this morning affecting all students . . ."

Somewhere in the distance a bell rang.

### Jesus wept

Having completed His first mission, Jesus promised to come back and finish the job, taking His people home and ending pain and pride forever. Prophecies point to an unparalleled promise. But how do we separate the hope . . . from the hype?

"Jerusalem, Jerusalem, the city that kills the prophets and stones those who are sent to it! How often have I desired to gather your children together as a hen gathers her brood under her wings, and you were not willing! See, your house is left to you, desolate. For I tell you, you will not see me again until you say, 'Blessed is the one who comes in the name of the Lord'" (Matt. 23:37-39, NRSV).

Jesus spoke those weeping words to a crowd gathered inside Jerusalem's Temple. His words would have given pause and concern to anyone, but as we often see in the Bible, His disciples were a little thick. As the crowd caught its breath and they strolled out again, one of the disciples—the Bible writers mercifully decline to name him—piped up:

"Look, Teacher, what large stones and what large buildings!"

It was the week of Jesus' crucifixion, and He was spending it in Jerusalem, communicating His wisdom as if He had no time to lose.

The Temple was not the first one in Jerusalem, for the Babylonians had destroyed Solomon's original Temple some 600 years before. The Jews had rebuilt it after their exile, and then, under the reign of Herod the Great, an astonishing amount of construction began again. Now the Temple had been under construction for about 50 years.

To the Jews, the Temple was the Statue of Liberty, Eiffel Tower, and Taj Mahal rolled into one. It was the symbol of their connection with God, their place as His chosen people. The Lord communicated with His people through the Temple services. The ancient Jewish historian Josephus compared the Temple's white stone walls to a snow-covered mountain. According to him, the stones that formed its walls were approximately 40 feet long, 15 feet high, and 20 feet deep. The structure was the pride and joy and glory of the nation . . . Yet Jesus said to His disciples, "See these stones? This is true—not one stone will be left stacked on another; they'll all come down."

Work would continue on the Temple for another 30 years—until A.D. 63. Just seven years later a Roman army, led by its general, Titus, destroyed the Temple as he crushed a Jewish rebellion.

Jesus now withdrew to the Mount of Olives, and the crowd seemed to know that He needed some space. Peter, James, Andrew, and John approached Him privately. "When is this going to happen?" they asked. "And how will we know You're about to come back and end everything?"

Jesus looked at each disciple. No matter what happened in the next few days, there was hope for these guys yet. Then He gave them a multipart warning and advice, covering both the Temple's fall and His second coming:

*False messiahs will surface.* Do not be deceived by someone who claims to represent Jesus but takes divine glory for himself. Some will have satanic power to perform incredible signs and wonders, but you'll know they're not Jesus, because His return will be known and seen by all—like lightning igniting the sky.

*Don't be alarmed when you hear about wars here or there.* There are plenty of wars to go around. Jesus is in control, but the end is yet to come.

*Famines and natural disasters will strike, but keep your head—that's only the beginning.* Whatever happens, focus on Jesus.

*Persecution looms ahead.* Jesus said that many will lose their lives for Him, and many will lose their faith and betray their former friends.

*Many false prophets will crop up.* They will claim to speak for God, but their words must be measured against God's Word. Although such false gospels would deceive many, God's people must hold on to the true.

*Many will lose their love, but the tried and true will be saved.* Jesus called His followers to love God and each other. They had no greater calling, for to do so was to keep His commandments.

*When you see prophecy fulfilled, flee Jerusalem.* Great suffering will afflict all who put themselves in harm's way, but God will save His children in the nick of time.

*Old Testament prophecies of signs in the sky will come true.* Historical records suggest some strange phenomena appeared in the sky in Jerusalem before it fell. We shouldn't be surprised if similar events happen again today.

What came true for Jerusalem will also occur for the whole world at the end. Keep your eyes peeled, your head straight, your thinking caps on, and your expectations at home.

## Blind dates

My college classmates and I sat around the resident assistant's dorm room for evening worship. He looked up from the blue paperback book he held in his hands. "I believe Jesus is coming very soon," he said. "The signs are all around us. In fact, I think He'll come before the year 2000."

I pondered my RA's words. *Why do people like to say "the year" 2000? When somebody asked me when I was going to graduate, I didn't say, "I'm gonna graduate in the year 1998." Although that does seem to rhyme, so maybe I should have . . .*

In life's blur of history quizzes, first kisses, and near misses, excitement about Jesus inevitably fizzles. But His promised return is no less sure, and the only sure cure is to keep looking to Him.

Jon Paulien writes that the important thing "is not how clear a picture of the future one can concoct but how clear a picture of Christ we can gain." Taste and see that God is good. Then share that goodness with others.

After explaining what to watch for, Jesus told His disciples four stories that show how we should live in the meantime. The first is your typical Goofus and Gallant tale about two servants, one faithful, one wicked. The master says "I'll be back," but our Goofus thinks he's got plenty of time to goof off, and starts beating his coworkers. Needless to say, his narrative doesn't end well. What's Jesus' point? As we wait for Jesus' return, how we treat other people shows how seriously we take it. If we shift our attention from Jesus to other people or priorities, we'll lose the plot.

The second tale is about 10 bridesmaids waiting for a wedding, and shows how hard it is to keep focused on Jesus' return. Indeed, every one of them falls asleep—yet when they awake, those who had planned ahead have the glow they need to keep going. For us, it's a deep relationship with Jesus that will aid us when the night is cold and dark—a relationship that each one of us must cultivate ourselves.

The third story involves three servants whose master gives them money—talents (a certain weight of gold or silver)—to use while he is gone. Two put the money to work, but the other buries it lest he lose it. Those who use their gifts are rewarded, while the fearful one loses out. What does that mean to you and me? While you're waiting for Jesus, use the gifts God gave you.

And last, Jesus told how on judgment day He'll thank His followers for taking such good care of Him—feeding Him when He was hungry, clothing Him when He was cold, welcoming Him when He was lonely. They'll sheepishly ask Him, "When did we do all that? We never saw You—we were just doing what we remembered You doing for people." Then He will declare, "Indeed—everything you did for others, you really did for Me."

As for everyone else, Jesus will say, "You ignored the needy—and that really gets My goat" (see Matt. 25:31-46).

Jon Paulien writes that how we treat others is the essence of watching for Jesus' return. The Bible teaches us about the end "not to satisfy our curiosity about the future but to teach us how to live" in the meantime.

Our faithfulness to God will be crucial in the end-time. But in the meantime, we're faithful to Him by being kind to others.

# The Fakers

## CHAPTER 16

*"Then the dragon was enraged at the woman and went off to make war against the rest of her offspring—those who obey God's commandments and hold to the testimony of Jesus" (Rev. 12:17).*

*P*rophecy used to leave me cold.

It was all too . . . mathematical. In classic x = y style, teachers and pastors taught me that this equaled that: This beast equaled that country. Those numbers equaled that date. That crazy action equaled that event. Before long I could tell anyone who cared to ask (not that anybody did) that the lamblike beast represented America and that 1260 prophetic days equaled 1260 years.

What nobody ever taught me, though, was what it all meant or why it mattered. They explained what things symbolized, but . . . so what? It was an x = y game ("the Big Dipper equals the eighth nation from the right"), but such dry formulas really didn't help me understand the Bible, God, or the gospel better.

Until I got to my theological seminary.

I went because God nudged me there, but I still thought it'd be more of the same ol' same ol', only this time in the dead languages Greek and Hebrew. I didn't expect to see everything I thought I knew turned inside out. And when it came to prophecy, my profs transformed the flat, two-dimensional factoids I'd grown up with into three-dimensional relevance I could groove to.

For example, for all the talk I'd heard about the symbolic beast that received a "deadly wound," nobody had ever pointed out that it was a counterfeit of Jesus, "the lamb that was slain." Or that the dragon is a counterfeit of God the Father. Or that the fall of Babylon in Revelation parallels Babylon's fall in the Old Testament. Or that since just about every verse in Revelation is rooted in the images and phrases of earlier texts, the key to understanding it is to plug into the Bible's 65 other books. Suddenly I was working with a brand-new component: context.

As a result I discovered that Bible prophecy is about more than proof texts and strange beasts. It isn't about "us versus them," merely a way to tell the holy from the heathen. Nor is it just a fun mental exercise for cryptic details. And it isn't just about crises, but about Christ.

Once I finished slapping my forehead, I began to see prophecy's true potential. It's packed full of insights into the gospel, the church, and God's character. And it's far more fascinating than it ever was before.

Revelation's prime purpose isn't just to warn us what will happen where and when. Rather it's all about Jesus, the Lamb that was slain.

The end of the world has always fascinated Christians—well, scratch "Christians" and make it "people in general." What's next? Is this life all there is? What happens at the end? Will the earth someday wobble off its axis and find itself swallowed by a dying sun? Or is the world's Creator going to toss out the old model and redo earth in perfection?

And yet Revelation can seem as meaningful as the phone book, unless we know what's going on.

Take those gnarly beasts you've probably seen on a few too many evangelistic pamphlets. Directly paralleling the Trinity, they clue us in to what to expect during Planet Earth's last gasps.

World history is full of pretenders to God's glory. Many religions and institutions have claimed to speak for Him, but they've distorted the gospel and misrepresented His character through the misuse of power, and warped His law through their own substitutions. They've demanded allegiance and devotion that only God deserves, oppressing those who choose to follow their own conscience. Revelation uses a woman to symbolize God's people—His church—pursued and persecuted by three beasts representing world powers.

You'll find those three beasts in Revelation 13 and 14. Here's the gang of three imposters, each representing a false political and/or spiritual power at work misrepresenting God:

*The dragon.* As the head of the group, he mimics God the Father.

*The sea beast.* He gets his authority from the dragon—just as Jesus received authority from His Father. Although killed, he yet lives—like Jesus. And as Jesus was on earth for three and a half literal years, the sea beast is allowed (Rev. 13:5) 42 months—a literal equivalent of three and a half years or 1260 prophetic days.

*The land beast.* You guessed it—the Holy Spirit. As the Holy Spirit took the place of Jesus after His return to heaven, so the land beast picks up where the sea beast left off. And like the Holy Spirit at Pentecost, the great reaping of believers 50 days after Jesus' resurrection, the land beast brings fire down from heaven. He will deceive many into thinking they're following God, even though they're accepting a satanic fraud.

Second Thessalonians tells a similar tale. "And then the lawless one will be revealed, whom the Lord Jesus will overthrow with the breath of his mouth and destroy by the splendor of his coming. The coming of the lawless one will be in accordance with the work of Satan displayed in all kinds of counterfeit miracles, signs, and wonders, and in every sort of evil that deceives those who are perishing" (2 Thess. 2:8-10).

Most Christians take Paul's statement as a description of the antichrist—an invincible devil incarnate who rules the world in the last days. The reality, however, is much more nuanced. The Bible's concept of antichrist goes far beyond that of a single individual. And since the Bible sees the last days as beginning with Jesus' resurrection, the spirit of antichrist has been active as long as Jesus has been proclaimed. The Bible actually uses the word "antichrist" only in two books, 1 and 2 John. Here's everything Scripture says about it:

"Dear children, this is the last hour; and as you have heard that the antichrist is coming, even now many antichrists have come. This is how we know it is the last hour . . . Who is the liar? It is the man who denies that Jesus is the Christ. Such a man is the antichrist—he denies the Father and the Son. No one who denies the Son has the Father; whoever acknowledges the Son has the Father also" (1 John 2:18-23).

"This is how you can recognize the Spirit of God: Every spirit that acknowledges that Jesus Christ has come in the flesh is from God, but every spirit that does not acknowledge Jesus is not from God. This is the spirit of the antichrist, which you have heard is coming and even now is already in the world" (1 John 4:2, 3).

"Many deceivers, who do not acknowledge Jesus Christ as coming in the flesh, have gone out into the world. Any such person is the deceiver and the antichrist" (2 John 1:7).

Even the word "antichrist" doesn't mean what many people assume. It does not stand for "against Christ" or "enemy of Christ," but rather "in place of Christ." Thus anything—whether doctrine, diva, or denomination—that substitutes the human for the divine, reflects the spirit of antichrist. From putting human works or rituals in place of Jesus' perfect sacrifice, to saying that we can somehow add our own merits to our salvation, to discouraging us from praying to Jesus, or to suggesting we can be self-sufficient—all mirror the antichrist's spirit. So if you're looking for the antichrist, don't search in *People* magazine, journey to a foreign country, or cross-examine another religion's leader—look in the mirror, and make sure that you have utterly given up your life to glorifying Jesus and following His Word.

Satan's final deceptions will be both subtle and awe-inspiring, but there will be nothing really new about them. You'll recognize his greatest hits: People can be like God on their own power. Death isn't final. God forces people to follow Him. Forget that the Lord is the one who created you.

How can you avoid being taken in by a league of fakers? The only way to know that the beasts aren't who they claim to be is to know God so intimately that you'd instantly recognize the diabolical difference.

**If looks could kill**

"You've gotta keep the commandments to be ready for the last days" was the message I heard growing up. What my teachers meant, though, was the commandments about worshipping God—worship God and no idols, speak no ill of

God, and honor God's Sabbath. Jesus summed those up as "Love the Lord your God with all your heart, and with all your soul, and with all your mind," calling it "the greatest and first commandment." Yet unlike my religion teachers, He didn't stop there. He continued, "And a second is like it: 'You shall love your neighbor as yourself'" (Matt. 22:37-39, NRSV).

The Pharisees were big on the Ten Commandments' Top Four, making sure that every outward appearance proclaimed that they worshipped God and kept the Sabbath spic and span. (And for good measure they were pretty strict about number 7, too—adultery.) Unfortunately, they seemed to find the other commandments a little slippery. Honor your parents? Jesus pointed out how they'd say, "Well, I'd love to support my parents in their old age, but I dedicated this money to God, so, sorry . . . I'll send a card at Hanukkah . . ." Don't murder? If looks could kill, Phil Pharisee would have been Jacob the Ripper. Don't tell a lie? They were living one. Don't steal? Their greed took advantage of the poor at every turn. Don't covet? Don't even go there . . .

Revelation 13 and 14 mention worship no less than eight times. With its images of false gods seeking worship (commandment number 1), people worshipping beastly images (number 2), blasphemy (number 3), and a command to worship the Creator of heaven and earth (number 4, the Sabbath), the book of Revelation makes it clear as the sea of glass that how we worship God will be at the center of earth's end-time crisis. Every human power will push us to break those first four commandments. When Revelation highlights the importance of worshipping God alone, it echoes the Old Testament's words about the Sabbath, the day in which believers can rest in God's completed work—a day of grace and good works for others—and remember that He alone is their Creator and Redeemer.

No concept in the book of Revelation has inspired people's imagination and speculation more than the mysterious and spooky "mark of the beast." Is it strictly symbolical? Or could it be something along the nature of a skin-embedded microchip or a satanic tattoo?

With God's commandments the central issue in Revelation 13 and 14, the mark's mission is clear: it parodies and subverts the Sabbath's blessings. The divine commandment says that "the *seventh* day is the Sabbath of God"; Revelation 13 talks about "the *number* of the beast." The Old Testament declares the Sabbath to be a day free of the commercialism of buying and selling; the mark of the beast punishes those who refuse to accept it by not allowing them to buy or sell at all. The Sabbath proclaims rest for son, daughter, slave, animal, and foreigner (Ex. 20:10); the beast forces its mark on "everyone, small and great, rich and poor, free and slave."

Whereas the Sabbath promises worldwide blessing, the beast's imitation brings a worldwide curse. Both restrict work, but one refreshes while the other punishes. The Sabbath offers rest, but the mark, like that placed on Cain after he kills his brother Abel, brings restlessness. As Anthony McPherson writes, "The Sabbath is willing obedience to the Creator God, but the mark works by a coercive force that achieves obedience through fear and deception (Rev. 13:13-17). Each one is a fitting sign, reflecting the nature of the giver. The mark is a sad and oppressive parody of the life-affirming gift of the Lord of the Sabbath." The contrast reveals the difference between the Creator God, who values our freedom and desires the best for us, and the coercive dragon, who uses force and control for his own personal intentions.

Which brings us back to another issue. Jesus makes it clear that we cannot fake our way into His kingdom. Relationship is what counts:

"Not everyone who says to me, 'Lord, Lord,' will enter the kingdom of heaven, but only the one who does the will of my Father in heaven. On that day many will say to me, 'Lord, Lord, did we not prophesy in your name, and cast out demons in your name, and do many deeds of power in your name?' Then I will declare to them, 'I never knew you; go away from me, you evildoers'" (Matt. 7:21-23, NRSV).

Love God. Love others. Yes, those are the issues in the last days. But they should also be how we should live today—and every day.

# Investigation Station

## CHAPTER 17

*"There's a man going' 'round takin' names.*
*And he decides who to free and who to blame.*
*Everybody won't be treated all the same.*
*There'll be a golden ladder reaching down.*
*When the man comes around."*—Johnny Cash,
*"The Man Comes Around."*

God promises to come and set everything right—but not all have chosen the right. How can He take eternal life from people while still assuring us of His love and fairness? By making sure that everything's "aboveboard." Again and again the Bible shows us Him bending over backward to ensure, and assure us, that His judgments are sound and true.

## Corrupt Sodom Investigation

After their meal Abraham walked alongside his guests as a good host would. He had offered them food and a spot to rest (as he would have any strangers traveling through a harsh land), yet there was something different about these three. They knew of his and Sarah's decades-long wish for a child, and they had made her laugh with their assurance that a year from then she'd at last have her own baby boy.

And indeed, the visitors were not ordinary at all.

One of them paused and looked at Abraham. "The outcry against Sodom and Gomorrah is so great," God said, "and their sin so grievous that I will go down and see if what they have done is as bad as the outcry that has reached me. If not, I will know" (Gen. 18:20, 21).

The patriarch's jaw dropped. It was too much. (A) This was clearly God standing before him, and (B) his nephew Lot lived in Sodom—and now God was about to destroy it?

Abraham watched as the two other men headed toward Sodom; then he sputtered, "Will You sweep away the righteous with the wicked? What if there are fifty righteous people in the city? Will You really sweep it away and not spare the place for the sake of the fifty righteous people in it? Far be it from you to do such a thing—to kill the righteous with the wicked, treating the righteous and the wicked alike. Far be it from you! Will not the Judge of all the earth do right?" (verses 23-25).

God said, "If I find fifty righteous people in the city of Sodom, I will spare the whole place for their sake" (verse 26).

Abraham's mind raced. Sodom was hardly Eden, but what if there were just 45? 40? 30? 20? 10? *Surely there are at least 10 decent people in Sodom.* After a few moments' discussion, God assured the stunned Abraham that yes, 10 people would be enough to spare the city. And Abraham left it at that.

Lot sat at the gate of his adopted city. He did not know that his uncle had just hosted three divine visitors—or that two of them were headed his way. Nonetheless, when he saw two out-of-towners approaching, he invited them to come over and rest a spell.

"No," they said, "we will spend the night in the square" (Gen. 19:2). But Lot insisted and showed them to his house, baking unleavened bread for them before they retired for the night.

And then the crowd materialized. A hysterical mob of men, young and old, shook the house with their ravings. "Send out those strangers!" they bellowed. "We're gonna ravage 'em!"

Stunned, Lot apparently said the first thing that popped into his head: "How 'bout my daughters instead?"

Clearly, if Lot was the best of the lot, Sodom was about to sizzle. Still, the angels had to yank him and his wife and kids out before the heavens opened, urging them to "flee for your lives! Don't look back!" (verse 17).

The investigation was complete. God was ready to act.

## Don't pass me by

The plagues on Egypt had gone on for weeks, from hail to darkness to dead livestock. Now, at last, the final one loomed over the nation. Soon God would set His people free.

Moses told the Hebrews to prepare bitter herbs and unleavened bread, to mark their doorways with a lamb's blood, and then shut themselves up inside their houses. That night the Lord would pass over their houses to investigate who trusted in the blood of a lamb. "The blood will be a sign for you on the houses where you are; and when I see the blood, I will pass over you" (Ex. 12:13).

God's following the same spiritual plan today, just as He always has. In the garden of Eden, He asked, "Where are you?" "Who told you that you were naked?" and "What is this you have done?" (Gen. 3:9-13). Before destroying the tower of Babel, "the Lord came down to look over the city and the tower those people had built" (Gen. 11:5, Message).

The Bible shows us that God always investigates before executing judgment. As we await Jesus' second coming, we can know and trust that the Lord will do everything in His power to save us. And because He wants the universe to understand both His love and His judgment, He makes sure that everything He does will be clear to all.

# Face to Face

## CHAPTER 18

*"In the womb he grasped his brother's heel; as a man he struggled with God. He struggled with the angel and overcame him; he wept and begged for his favor" (Hosea 12:3, 4).*

*"But who can endure the day of his coming? Who can stand when he appears? For he will be like a refiner's fire or a launderer's soap" (Mal. 3:2).*

*"Now we see but a poor reflection as in a mirror; then we shall see face to face. Now I know in part; then I shall know fully, even as I am fully known."—Paul (1 Cor. 13:12).*

*A*thletes are notorious for their pregame rituals. Tap the locker room ceiling before heading out to the field. Scuff the dirt at home plate three times. Wear something lucky. For soccer player Adam Bruckner, things were a little more complicated.

Thoughts of tragedy and death dogged his days. An obsessive fixation on "good" and "bad" numbers compelled him to count his steps or the number of times he flipped a light switch. *Three for luck, five for keeping my health, eight for keeping my mom safe,* he'd think. *Can't stop at four switches or I'll bust my knee and end my soccer career, and Mom might die.* Fearing a world out of balance, he'd touch every tree he passed, count incessantly, and save every bottle of Gatorade he drank, stacking them to his ceiling along two walls of his bedroom.

Single and out of college after playing Division I soccer in school, Bruckner hoped to go pro, but breaks didn't last. For three years he chased his dream, hitting tryout after tryout in city after city, from Biloxi to Baltimore, Phoenix to Detroit. Somehow the lifestyle attracted him. Adrift yet curious, he felt a connection with the homeless, whose only roots were things they could hoard. People used to being passed over found kinship with Bruckner. They'd ask him for spare change, and he'd request their story—over dinner. Bruckner wrote their tales down in his journal, narratives of true bad luck and misfortune, mental illness and addiction.

Soon Bruckner began to see new patterns—patterns formed not by arbitrary numbers, but by human connections, of disparate people—on the train, on the road—witnessing about God's power and love. It had been years since he'd so much as picked up a Bible, but their messages and that of others assured him that life was neither meaningless nor so perilous as he imagined.

One day in Baltimore, where he was training with the Baltimore Blast, Bruckner headed to a gym to work out. Suddenly a light pole obsessed him. He needed to touch it, had to caress it before walking past, or—face disaster. Fate seemed to depend on his next move.

But this time was different. New words formed in his brain, broke through to his lips: "Trust God, and you'll be all right."

Bruckner walked on, leaving the light pole untouched. He was surprised to feel not fear, but freedom. A new sense of liberation took over, and he poured his energies outward. Praying for God to use him, he volunteered in homeless shelters and church outreach ministries. Passing out sandwiches led to more concentrated forms of help for others. He's written countless checks made out to state agencies so people can obtain birth certificates and ID cards necessary to apply for jobs as truck drivers or fast-food handlers. Today, while a coach for the Philadelphia KiXX, he devotes spare time to cooking at Philadelphia's Helping Hands Rescue Mission, and speaks to area youth groups. People who say his aid turned their lives around regularly approach him to express their thanks.★

## Fear or Friendship

Fear. It's as old as Eden, as human as hunger. And for many it's the very foundation of religion. With the idea of judgment drawing nigh, God's a pretty scary guy. He is holiness and perfection while I can barely keep track of my car keys.

Fear rules our culture. The evening news blares new reasons to worry about things we might take for granted. Politicians tell us that terrorists may attack us if we vote for the wrong candidate. Too often we fear the wrong things for the wrong reasons, being traumatized by commercial air travel (by far the safest form of transportation) but never worrying when we sit down in a car. We fear strangers, when more than 80 percent of crimes are perpetrated by people the victim knows. The fear of exotic diseases distracts us, while diabetes creeps up on us. Fear sells newspapers, and the news exploits our fears, while we all look in the wrong direction.

Abraham's grandson Jacob had plenty of reasons to be afraid. He'd just agreed to a truce with Laban, his conniving father-in-law, but now the day he truly dreaded loomed in front of him. Two decades before, he'd cheated his twin brother, Esau, out of the patriarchal blessing due him, tricking their blind father by dressing in Esau's clothes and serving his brother's food. He'd split town and hustled to his mother's family, but now the brothers would meet again. Esau was a man of the land, long of hair but short of temper. Did he still hold a grudge? Would he meet Jacob with a homegrown army and slaughter Jacob and enslave his children? Jacob had no way to know. He only knew he couldn't run anymore, and God was bidding him home.

A few marital mix-ups aside, the years away had been good to Jacob. God had prospered him with wealth and children, sheep and cattle. Now Jacob sent messengers ahead to assure Esau of his goodwill. "Tell Esau his servant Jacob is coming," he instructed. "Tell him I've been staying with Laban, and now have cattle and donkeys, sheep and goats, menservants and maidservants. Now I am sending this message to my lord, that I may find favor in your eyes."

The men returned with a bit of mixed message. They'd seen Esau, all right, and he was headed this way to meet them—with 400 armed mercenaries.

Jacob did his best not to panic. He decided to divide everything and everybody with him into two groups, thinking, *If Esau comes and attacks one group, the group that is left may escape.* Then he poured his heart out to God with the honesty he'd so long lacked:

"O God of my father Abraham, God of my father Isaac, O Lord, who said to me, 'Go back to your country and your relatives, and I will make you prosper,' I am unworthy of all the kindness and faithfulness you have shown your servant. I had only my staff when I crossed this Jordan, but now I have become two groups. Save me, I pray, from the hand of my brother Esau, for I am afraid he will come and attack me, and also the mothers with their children. But you have said, 'I will surely make you prosper and will make your descendants like the sand of the sea, which cannot be counted'" (Gen. 32:9-12).

Deciding that a peace offering was his best hope, Jacob sent messengers again, along with more than 500 animals to offer Esau. "Tell him they belong to his servant Jacob," he said. "They're a gift to his lord Esau."

That night Jacob sent his family across a stream, but stayed behind by himself. Sleep eluded his racing mind. He could think of nothing but how wrong he'd been to steal what God would have freely given, and of the consequences he couldn't escape. It had robbed him of relationships with family and friends, and now that same sin could destroy him and all that he loved. He poured out his heart to God, his only hope. *Rescue me! Forgive me!*

Suddenly a man attacked him in the darkness. Jacob's feet slipped on the ground as he fought back. Who was this? The darkness hid everything but the man's muscular grip. Was it Esau come to kill him? one of Esau's hired goons? a robber? a wild animal that only felt like a man? As Jacob wrestled in the silence of the night, drenched in mud and sweat, he felt that everything in his life had led up to this moment of struggle.

The night dragged on, filled with twisting and turning, groaning and grunting, and he could no longer tell if they'd wrestled for an hour or six hours. Suddenly the attacker touched his thigh, and pain shot through Jacob's body. Now Jacob knew—this was no ordinary man.

"Let me go, for it is daybreak," the man said, the first words either had spoken all night. But despite the shockwaves of agony coursing through him, Jacob held on. He sensed that somehow God was giving him a second chance. Stealing his father's blessing had cursed him, but this would be different.

"I will not let you go," Jacob insisted, wrapping his arms yet tighter around the other's body, "unless you bless me."

"What is your name?" the man asked, steadying Jacob's limp legs.

"Jacob," he gasped. He knew that his name sounded like the word for *heel grasper*. His mother had given him that name after he'd come into the world with his hands wrapped around his brother's foot. The double meaning of the words had been all too fitting, for a "heel grasper" was a deceiver, one who tried to take credit for another's work.

The man at last looked Jacob in the eyes. "Your name will no longer be Jacob, but Israel, because you have struggled with God and with men and have overcome."

"Please tell me your name," Jacob begged.

"Why do you ask my name?" the person asked, and at last gave Jacob the blessing he'd longed for. As the man vanished into the sunrise, Jacob marveled as he took a moment to rest. He decided to call the place Peniel—face of God. "I saw God face to face, and yet my life was spared" (verses 26-30).

That day Jacob and Esau fell upon each other—not in battle, but in embrace; to shed not blood, but tears. And Jacob declared that with such undeserved grace from his once-estranged brother, seeing Esau's face was like viewing the face of God.

Without a repentant heart, Jacob could not have survived his encounter with God. Like the wicked at Jesus' return destroyed "by the splendor of His coming" (2 Thess. 2:8), Jacob would have been lost. But God knew that the man regretted his actions, and His grace counted Jacob as if he'd never sinned.

**"Fear not"**

Whenever someone supernatural shows up in the Bible, you can count on

134

the words "Fear not." Something about the godly turns our legs to jelly. Even Moses hid his face in terror, afraid to look at God, once he realized that the mysteriously burning bush contained the Creator.

When God appeared at Mount Sinai, his glory blazing like a fire on the top of the mountain, His voice echoing across the valley, the Israelites recoiled with fear and kept their distance. They asked Moses to mediate between them and God: "Speak to us yourself and we will listen. But do not have God speak to us or we will die" (Ex. 20:19). Now it was Moses' turn to say, "Don't be afraid." Then he went up the mountain to commune with God by himself.

When Moses hiked back down after spending 40 days with the Almighty, the sight of him freaked the people out. Moses' face still glowed from his one-on-one with Yahweh. So Moses courteously wore a veil over his face, taking it off only when God's pillar of fire came down to His "tent of meeting" and Moses returned to God's presence. About those chitchats the Bible says, "The Lord would speak to Moses face to face, as a man speaks with his friend" (Ex. 33:11).

Even after three years of hanging out with and learning from Jesus, Jesus' disciples still feared God the Father. Sitting around the upper room after their last dinner before Jesus' death, Jesus promised His disciples that He'd return for them, and told them to put their trust in God. "You know the way to the place where I am going," He said.

Thomas started in his seat. "Lord," he said, "we don't know where you are going, so how can we know the way?"

Jesus looked him in the eye. "I am the way and the truth and the life. No one comes to the Father except through me. If you really knew me, you would know my Father as well. From now on, you do know him and have seen him."

Philip could hardly contain himself at these words. "Lord," he pleaded, "show us the Father and that will be enough for us."

"Don't you know me, Philip, even after I have been among you such a long time? Anyone who has seen me has seen the Father." Jesus explained that He and God were one, and that God worked through Him. Indeed, anyone who put faith in Jesus would do the same work through God's power. "And I will do whatever you ask in my name, so that the son may bring glory to the Father," Jesus said. "You may ask me for anything in my name, and I will do it" (John 14:4-9) "I no longer call you servants," Jesus said, "because a servant does not know his master's business. Instead, I have called you friends, for everything that I learned from my Father I have made known to you" (John 15:15).

It was quite the promise, but the promises weren't over yet. Jesus assured His followers that they would have a relationship with God like the one that Moses had enjoyed. Though Moses had interceded with God for the Israelites, and now Jesus promised to take our requests to God, Jesus spoke of a time to come when He will no longer need to mediate between the human race and God. "In that day you will ask in my name. I am not saying that I will ask the Father on your behalf. No, the Father himself loves you" (John 16:26, 27).

### Jacob's trouble

"At that time Michael, the great prince, the protector of your people, shall arise. There shall be a time of great anguish, such as has never occurred since nations came into existence. But at that time your people shall be delivered, everyone who is found written in the book" (Dan. 12:1, NRSV).

For many no doctrine has inspired fear quite like that of the "time of trouble"—fear of somehow losing salvation in God's judgment, and fear of who knows what physical and psychological duress. But we can take comfort in Jacob's experience wrestling with God. As Jeremiah wrote:

> "Cries of fear are heard—
> terror, not peace.
>
> "Ask and see:
> Can a man bear children?
> Then why do I see every strong man
> with his hands on his stomach like a woman in labor,
> every face turned deathly pale?
>
> "How awful that day will be!
> None will be like it.
> It will be a time of trouble for Jacob,
> but he will be saved out of it" (Jer. 30:5-7).

The day is coming when God will declare, "Let him who does wrong continue to do wrong; let him who is vile continue to be vile; let him who does right continue to do right; and let him who is holy continue to be holy" (Rev. 22:11). Jesus' work as mediator will be finished. The Holy Spirit's work on our hearts is over. Then salvation or damnation will be decided for everyone, and the "time of trouble" Daniel spoke of will begin.

As this world ends, terror surrounds us, our sins seem too great to be forgiven, and we'll cling to God the way Jacob did on that long-ago night. Nothing we can do can merit forgiveness, but we can depend on Jesus' forgiveness and atonement. As we wrestle with God, He will change our hearts forever.

Like Jacob, like Moses, we will know God face to face. The divine presence is awesome and terrifying. The light of God's glory will destroy all who have not put their faith in Him. But to all who claim forgiveness through Jesus' sacrifice, God's glory is "like a refiner's fire," transforming us into His own image.

When God looks at us that day, He'll see not a broken sinner, but His perfect child. He'll gaze at us with love and affection and declare, "This is my beloved son, my beloved daughter, in whom I am well pleased."

*"How great is the love the Father has lavished on us, that we should be called children of God! And that is what we are! The reason the world does not know us is that it did not know him. Dear friends, now we are children of God, and what we will be has not yet been made known. But we know that when he appears, we shall be like him, for we shall see him as he is. Everyone who has this hope in him purifies himself, just as he is pure"* (1 John 3:1-3).

---

*Adapted from "End of the Trail," *ESPN,* Nov. 7, 2005.

# Aquatic Revelation

## CHAPTER 19

*"Listen, I tell you a mystery . . . the perishable must clothe itself with the imperishable, and the mortal with immortality."*
—Paul (1 Cor. 15:51-53).

A smooth motorboat ride zipped us from one pier to another on the Caribbean shore of Roatan in the Bay Islands. At just 9:00 in the morning we found the beach still empty of people. On Sunday we'd fly back to San Pedro Sula, Honduras, to construct churches and give medical aid in the continuing aftermath of Hurricane Mitch, but today was Friday, and recreation was in store.

Alighting on shore, I watched my friends Vickie, Toni, and Tim slap on sunscreen, slip into flippers and masks, and step into the sea. They floated away, noses in the water, flippers flapping behind them.

Meanwhile, with the words *This is the life* slipping through my brain, and my toes burrowing in soft sand, I leaned back under a tree for some much-needed rest and relaxation. The sun sparkled through the palm fronds above me as the cyan sea gently lapped the beach. I wrote in my notebook and gazed out at the water and hills. In the distance my friends bobbed on the water, peering at a world I'd never seen.

# Things They Never Taught Me

"You ready to try it, Tompaul?"

I looked up. Tim, a creature from the blue lagoon, dripping salt water, with flippered feet and a snorkel in one hand, stood smiling before me. "Well . . ." I sputtered. "Um . . . I've always wanted to. I would if I could swim."

"No problem," he replied. "The water's so salty you can just float on it."

I wasn't so sure. I've never swum an inch. I can't even dog-paddle. And as for floating, I might as well have rocks for bones. But Tim wouldn't give up. "Here—try on these goggles," he offered.

Still I hesitated. Sinking, grasping, sputtering, spluttering—a dozen memories of submerged panic gurgled through my mind. I swallowed. Maybe it'd be like all those joyous, buoyous pictures of tourists in the Dead Sea, willing themselves to sink but gleefully failing. "O . . . K . . . Sure . . ."

Before I knew it, I'd stowed my watch in a shoe, slathered fresh sunblock on my back, and squeezed into flippers. Reluctantly I waddled toward the water. Then into it.

Tim helped me adjust the mask, and I chomped down on the mouthpiece, preparing to choke at any moment. But I didn't choke, so I dared to take the next step—breathing underwater. My friend showed me how to clear the tube when necessary, and I dipped below the surface. Although I was standing in water only up to my knees, I wanted to make sure that I could breathe here. If so, I could breathe anywhere, right?

Now for the next trick—floating. A few false starts later, and sure enough, the salt water buoyed me like a twig. *So far, so good,* I thought. *Now to ignore the perils and head on out.* Lying on my stomach, propelled by limbs, flippers, and willpower, I left the shore behind.

Instantly my whole world changed. As Tim and I floated out farther and farther, I could scarcely believe this new reality that now seemed so natural. I felt as if I'd always lived and breathed underwater. Floating was as effortless as walking. The water and fish surrounding me seemed as normal as air and birds would be on land.

I chortled in sudden, joyous astonishment. A bright-orange fish with purple highlights glided by. It appeared the silliest and most beautiful thing I'd ever seen.

Twice in my underwater exploration I thought, *Hey, I'm floating over water I can drown in. This is—this is bizarre!* And twice I had to come up for air and reorient myself. But each time it was easier to slip back into my underwater mode.

At last I reached the coral, encountering underwater creatures of such startling exquisiteness that I couldn't help laughing again. A year before I'd waded through coral and skewered my leg on a jagged branch. Now a sunflower-yellow fish with big round white eyes swam behind a rock, while an electric-blue fish minded its own wet business beside me. It seemed that a child's box of paints and crayons had spilled into water, formed shapes, and burst to radiant life. Immersed in a kaleidoscope of nature, I felt as if I'd fallen into the sky and discovered jewels and rainbows wandering by.

Never before had I experienced such a world, one so alien to everything I took for granted, yet one that couldn't have felt more natural.

When Jesus comes back for us in the clouds, we'll change "in a flash, in the twinkling of an eye, at the last trumpet. For the trumpet will sound, the dead will be raised imperishable, and we will be changed" (1 Cor. 15:52).

Though our feet have always been stuck to the ground, at that time nothing will seem more normal than to forget gravity and soar up to Jesus.

# Your Lips, God's Ears

## CHAPTER 20

*"O Lord, hear my prayer, listen to my cry for mercy; in your faithfulness and righteousness come to my relief."—David (Ps. 143:1).*

*"He will respond to the prayer of the destitute; he will not despise their plea." (Ps. 102:17).*

*"If you believe, you will receive whatever you ask for in prayer." —Jesus, (Matt. 21:22).*

*"Watch and pray so that you will not fall into temptation. The spirit is willing, but the body is weak."—Jesus, (Matt. 26:41).*

*"And pray in the Spirit on all occasions with all kinds of prayers and requests. With this in mind, be alert and always keep on praying for all the saints."—Paul (Eph. 6:18).*

As soon as 2-year-old Lisa learned how to pray, she prayed religiously for four things: that she would go to sleep fast, that she would wake up the right time in the morning, that she would not have any bad dreams—and that God would send her a brother and a sister. Every time her parents asked her to pray, whether at mealtime or bedtime, she asked God for a brother and sister. Years went by, and in vain her parents explained that "Mommy's getting older and we haven't had another child yet, so there may not be any more children."

"But Mommy," Lisa said, "Sarah was 99 years old, and she had a baby." In her mind there was no question—God would answer her prayer.

Around Lisa's sixth birthday her mother came down with what at first seemed like a wicked case of the flu. Then, a few days later Lisa's mother picked her up from kindergarten and said, "Mommy's pregnant. You're going to have a brother or a sister."

"I get a brother and a sister!" her daughter squealed.

"No, I'm only pregnant with one," her mother said.

"You'll have two," Lisa declared. "Jesus answered my prayer."

The sonogram revealed twins.

The pregnancy was not without complications. Lisa's mother had to remain bedridden the latter part of the pregnancy, so the child would come in to her mother's room and talk to her and the invisible babies. A few days before the delivery Lisa's mother was admitted to the hospital, and the doctors conducted one more sonogram. They could tell that one baby was a boy, but the other remained a mystery.

Lisa's parents bought her a set of Cabbage Patch dolls, a boy and a girl, to give to her after the babies were born. The day Lisa's mother gave birth her father called the girl from the hospital. "Lisa," he said, "you now have two brothers."

"Daddy, are you kidding me?"

"No, I'm serious, Lisa. Mommy had two little boys—Michael and Matthew."

Her parents asked her if she'd like the original dolls they'd bought her, or if she'd like two boy dolls. "I want two boys," she said. "Just like Mommy."

Today Lisa feels that God answered her prayer—not exactly as she requested, but according to His design. In her childlike faith she had never doubted, and she never grew tired of waiting. To this day she delights in her brothers as God's gift to her family.

## Have a little talk with Jesus

I think that if I understood prayer I might understand God.

Prayer is a mystery. I believe it's opened hearts and changed history, but like anything connected with God, pinning down how it "works" isn't so easy. Even an abstract concept such as "love" seems easier to explain. What is prayer—just a spiritual discipline? a statistical boost that makes miracles more likely? a way to keep God from forgetting about us?

When Elijah challenged the prophets of Baal to a fire-from-heaven contest, he gave them a gentlemanly head start. The false prophets danced ever more wildly around their Baal altar, tearing off their clothes, slicing open their flesh in desperate attempts to get their deity's attention. Elijah egged them on: "Perhaps he is deep in thought, or busy, or traveling. Maybe he is sleeping and must be awakened" (1 Kings 18:27).

But the Bible assures us that God isn't like that. We don't need to beat His door down to get His attention, and no theatrics are necessary—yet Jesus "offered up prayers and petitions with loud cries and tears to the one who could save him from death, and he was heard because of his reverent submission" (Heb. 5:7).

People pray for all manner of things and reasons. There are wishes: "God, help him make that field goal." There are life's pressing needs and urgent prayers for intervention: "Help me make this month's mortgage payment." "Lord, heal that child's brain tumor."

We pray for long-term things: "I want to be a lawyer." We pray for relationships: "Jesus, help him to forgive me. Help me to forgive him." We pray for world leaders, for protection from disaster, for God to reshape our characters, for others to hear His voice.

Prayer is simple when you break it down—just talk to God—yet the implications of it are so immense (and perhaps even frightening). But while there are many styles and ways and forms and settings of prayer, the most important thing is just to pray. Maintain that connection with God. Keep the conversation open.

Sometimes we may begin to think of prayer as a form of magic, as if God is a computer waiting for the right password, or someone we can manipulate in some way. Nor is the purpose of prayer to justify yourself before God. God knows you. He understands you. The Lord just wants your heart—nothing more, and nothing less.

Often we think God listens only to certain kinds of prayers, yet the Bible paints a much different picture, including prayers of complaint and criticism that seem almost sacrilegious. The appropriately titled book of Lamentations moans:

> "He has made me dwell in darkness like those long dead.
> He has walled me in so I cannot escape;
>   he has weighed me down with chains.
> Even when I call out or cry for help,
>   he shuts out my prayer" (Lam. 3:6-8).

As in any good conversation, God wants our honesty. If you're frustrated that things just keep getting worse, tell Him! Explain why you're mad at Him. Admit to Him why you can't just take it anymore.

Out of the agony of Lamentations' grievance, just a few lines later, we find these words of promise:

"Yet this I call to mind
   and therefore I have hope:
Because of the Lord's great love we are not consumed,
   for his compassions never fail.
They are new every morning;
   great is your faithfulness" (verses 21-23).

When I read those words, I hear music—not because it's so beautiful, but because somebody's actually put those words to music and I've heard it played lots of times in church. Yet for some reason nobody seems to have written a song for verses 6-8. Maybe someone should. God loves to hear our praise, but He also wants our prayers to be real.

Prayer can feel presumptuous. Why should God ever answer my prayer? At any given moment countless people find themselves getting crushed by life—mothers dying, children crying, all while, as the psalmists note, the wicked do pretty well. Who can understand the mind of God? But in prayer you pour out all the reasons you think something should or should not be, and then you can have the peace that comes from knowing that you've said all there is to say and that God will take care of it. And even though you know He will take care of it, it doesn't mean you skip going over the reasons. Prayer reminds us of how dependent we are on Him and helps us face the world even when He doesn't automatically solve all our problems. It keeps us connected.

There's something about public prayers, though, that sometimes disturbs me. I stepped into my private Christian high school's campus church one sunny morning just in time to hear one of my teachers intone, "Lord, forgive us for our sins—and You know that some here especially need it." Ouch—no "present company excepted" there.

A few years later my sister and I drove up to our college campus church, our radio tuned to a broadcast of that morning's first service. As we started the mile-long drive a speaker was just getting started on a mile-long prayer. He seemed to be pondering and dissecting each of the Ten Commandments in elaborate and dramatic succession. Bronwen and I walked into church just in time to find the same speaker encoring his prayer for the second service, from the top.

The Bible's full of some crazy prayers, too. Consider Pharaoh's: "Get these frogs away from me!" (see Ex. 8:8). Then there's Hannah, who wept and prayed with "bitterness of soul" (1 Sam. 1:10) for God to give her a child—and had the high priest convinced that she must be drunk. But Hannah got her child, the high priest got a divine warning, and the Israelites got a leader in Samuel.

Prayer has power. We can't predict its effects—but don't underestimate it. We can't bottle it, but its power is unlimited. Paul wrote that God is "able to do immeasurably more than all we ask or imagine, according to his power that is at work within us" (Eph. 3:20).

Jesus said, "Ask and it will be given to you; seek and you will find; knock and the door will be opened to you. For everyone who asks receives; he who seeks finds; and to him who knocks, the door will be opened" (Luke 11:9, 10). While God has answered that prayer in countless ways, a few verses later Jesus makes clear the gift that God most longs to give us: the Holy Spirit.

*Prayer demands honesty—especially self-honesty.* Always remember that God knows all about you. But that's liberating, because you safely can be honest in front of Him.

Prayer recognizes that without God, we're nothing. Our best-intended actions are futile without His blessing. Yet it's easy to get caught up in our successes and forget to thank God. True prayer springs from gratitude and humility.

Prayers aren't for impressing people. God knows your heart and your motives. You can't fool Him with false piety, and public prayers aren't our chance to strut our spirituality. Jesus condemned the power brokers who "devour widows' houses and for a show make lengthy prayers" (Mark 12:40).

Today's politicians sometimes insist on turning prayer—and numerous other Christian essentials—into a political football, trying to make prayer a function of worldly government. Such actions rob prayer of its essential nature as a voluntary exercise by people genuinely seeking God.

*Prayer is our safeguard against sin.* The human will can be powerful, but apart from God it is ultimately weak. We're born broken. My father's father lived life on his own terms, and even willed himself free of cigarette addiction "cold turkey," but it took prayer and God's power to free him from bitterness. As people get on our nerves, as pale imitations of grace attract us, and as we start accepting false pictures of both ourselves and God, prayer orients and anchors us. It reminds us that no matter what we face, God is in ultimate control and will set all things right and make all things new—including our hearts.

Prayer gives us strength to face the world more than it saves us from it. Before He died Jesus prayed for His disciples: "My prayer is not that you take them out of the world but that you protect them from the evil one" (John 17:15).

*Prayer is especially necessary on behalf of those who hurt us.* My father shut his own father out of sight and mind for many years, coping with a childhood of hurt by focusing his thoughts elsewhere. When the Holy Spirit urged my father to pray for his father, he reluctantly assented—and the family soon saw the Spirit's impact on Grandpa Wheeler as well. As God chooses to use our actions to bless others, so He also employs our prayers. Sometimes our prayers are necessary to keep our affronted attitudes from obstructing the proud and spiritually weak. Often God urges us to pray for those who most offend us: "Pray for those who mistreat you" (Luke 6:28). Only the Holy Spirit can foster true reconciliation.

*Prayer can change hearts.* My great-grandmother, Mama Neff, was as busy as ever around her kitchen when a strange thought invaded her mind: *Pray for Allen.*

She tossed off the thought and continued with her work. Pray for Allen? Whatever for?

Allen was her son-in-law—well, her ex-son-in-law. Her mind skipped back, and she saw the man who'd married her daughter Isobel so many years before. "He was such a good-looking young man," she often said. But those days were long gone. Years of dissipation had left their mark on his bloated face. He was the worst kind of alcoholic—violent, cruel. As the years passed she'd grown to fear and hate the man who did such terrible things to his wife and children, the man who—at the end—had told Isobel in detail just how and where he planned to kill her and leave her body.

Only then did his wife find the courage to ask for help. Escaping with her two small children, she'd moved 1,000 miles away. How her mother missed her. How she prayed for them all. Time had passed. Isobel had found a decent job. The kids were thriving in their peaceful home. They were all doing well.

*Pray for Allen.*

Mama Neff wondered what was going on in his life. His parents still had some contact with Isobel and their grandchildren. She'd heard that he'd remarried, and had shaken her head at that. Oh, no. No! But the anger, the hurt, that she'd endured so long had mostly gone. If she felt anything toward the man it was sadness at what his life had been, and sorrow for what he'd once had, so foolishly drunk away.

*Pray for Allen!*

It was more than a thought. It was a command. Insistent. Almost demanding. Pray for . . .

She lifted her hands from the bread dough she was kneading. Quickly stripping her fingers of flour, she rinsed her hands, dried them, and strode to the adjoining dining room. There she knelt down by a chair, folded her hands, and prayed for this man she hadn't seen in years—father to three of her grandchildren, a lost yet cherished soul like anybody else.

Three days later someone found Allen's body in a room in a rundown hotel. His watch and Masonic ring were missing, probably stolen after his death. Medical examiners estimated that he had been dead three days. Cause of death: the effects on his body of decades of alcohol abuse.

Allen's parents took great comfort in the fact that there was no alcohol in his blood. Some time before, he'd told them that he'd quit drinking. It must be true, they told each other. It must be true.

Pray for Allen.

Why the thought? Why the command?

What is prayer about? How can we understand it?

Was the prayer for Mama Neff, or was it for Allen? Or was it for them both and the family who'd hear the story with wonder?

The Bible gives us some clues. In Job 42:8 God speaks to Job's three "comforters"—as in, "With comforters like those, who needs affliction?" God says, "My servant Job will pray for you, and I will accept his prayer and not deal with you according to your folly." Verse 9 adds: "And the Lord accepted Job's prayer."

No prayer is more mysterious than intercessory prayer. How is it that God needs our prayers to reach other people? Why not just act on His own initiative? Yet John wrote, "If anyone sees his brother commit a sin that does not lead to death, he should pray and God will give him life" (1 John 5:16). God chooses to use our prayers to bless others, even those struggling with sin and doubt and deception. It's a privilege we need to exercise more.

*Prayer brings people together.* I once prayed in a crowd of 10,000 people for an infant struggling for life, and who died just hours later. While God still allows tragedy, prayer unites us and reminds us that we're part of a greater universe of His design and love.

*Prayer is a lifestyle.* Paul's advice to "pray without ceasing" (1 Thess. 5:17, KJV) is both metaphor and mandate. Our sustaining connection with God keeps us in tune with His Spirit and will for us, and fuels our faith.

Paul wrote, "Do not be anxious about anything, but in everything, by prayer and petition, with thanksgiving, present your requests to God" (Phil. 4:6).

*Nothing is too big or small for prayer.* A college classmate of mine had returned to school after working maintenance many years. She sensed God's leading, but money was tight and the expenses of quitting her job, moving, and starting school would be high. Life had always been a struggle for her, but she clung to the promise of prayer. She confided in a friend, "I'm praying for an inexpensive used car without a lot of miles on it."

Her friend, though a strong Christian herself and someone normally reliable for sound spiritual advice, was nonplussed. "You can't pray for a car! That's not the kind of prayer God answers."

My friend found a car at a Saturn dealership that was perfect for her: previously owned by an elderly man who—you guessed it—literally drove it only to and from church and the grocery store, yet changed the oil and spark plugs as regularly as if he drove for a living. My friend's prayer had two answers—the car itself, and encouragement in God's leading and care.

*Sometimes the greatest prayer is letting go.*

# Stoking the Flame

## CHAPTER 21

*"You will seek me and find me when you seek me with all your heart"—God (Jer. 29:13).*

**W**elcome to the end of this book. How can you keep growing closer to God? Here are a few of my own ideas. You're sure to find some even better ones of your own.

*1. Listen to those who knew Him best.* The Bible's a big, bulky book. That's why it's good to work from the inside out. At the center of Scripture is—you guessed it—Jesus. With a story and life like no other, He is the one to dwell on. So pray for the Holy Spirit's guidance, then begin with the Gospels.

Keep asking yourself questions as you read: What motivated Jesus? What did He most value? What were His standards? How did He keep His connection with the Father?

As you explore the four Gospels, you'll soon discover that each one brings out a different fragment of the divine spectrum. Enjoy the colors.

*2. Find music that moves you spiritually.* Listen to examples that people have dedicated to God's glory. And see the difference it makes in your life.

*3. Pray as though you know Him.* Tell Jesus what's really on your mind—those extra pounds that bug you, the teacher who disrespects you, the friend who's stopped listening.

To read some honest dialogue with God, check out the Psalms, Job, or Lamentations. You'll find that along with the pomp and the praise, King David, Job, and other friends of God liked to tell Him what was on their minds (including their confusion, anger, or despair). Why? Because they knew that God was listening and that He'd answer.

Prayer helps you look at life through God's perspective, and suddenly the implausible becomes possible. And be prepared—your faith will grow.

*4. Put a Bible in the bathroom.* Find God in the in-between times and keep His Word close. You can also get audio editions, and let its words sink it in as you go here and there. (I've got Johnny Cash reading me the New Testament as I drive my car.) Then try to remember what you read or heard. If you can't, give God's Word a second or even fourth look.

*5. Put yourself in the picture.* Could you have been as patient as Job? How did Moses deal with doubt? What music would suit the Psalms? How does water feel under your feet when you walk on it? Ask the Holy Spirit to make the Bible real to you.

*6. Brush up on the Bible era.* A good Bible commentary can point out background info that brings new meaning to God's Word 3,000 years after writers first put pen to papyrus.

*7. Talk about it.* No two people ever experience God the very same way. So share what you're learning, seeing, and feeling. And listen to other people's perspectives. Also, read what other Christians have written, but never let that substitute for your own relationship with the Holy Spirit.

   8. *Look for God in the everyday.* He isn't confined by leather or red letters. Pause any way you can, and let Him blaze through the events of your life.

# Step inside a charismatic church . . . as an Adventist.

Seth, an Adventist preacher's kid, did just that—and ended up attending a Pentecostal church exclusively. Find out what he learned that every Christian should know. And discover how—in the midst of great music, rich worship, and deep fellowship—a still small voice convicted Seth to return to the church of his youth.

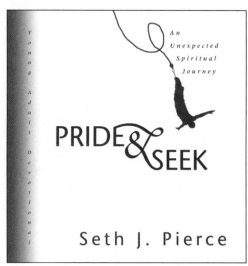

0-8280-1906-1. Paperback, 203 pages.

**3 Ways to Shop**
- Visit your local Adventist Book Center®.
- Call 1-800-765-6955.
- Order online at www.AdventistBookCenter.com.

REVIEW AND HERALD® PUBLISHING ASSOCIATION

Price and availability subject to change. Add GST in Canada.

# Been hit with detours in life?

Maybe those roadblocks aren't just coincidence. Maybe they are God's way of redirecting your route—or getting your attention. Journey with Larry Yeagley as he shares personal stories about life's little surprises and the lessons learned along the way. His lighthearted perspective is sure to leave you rethinking the twists and turns of everyday life.

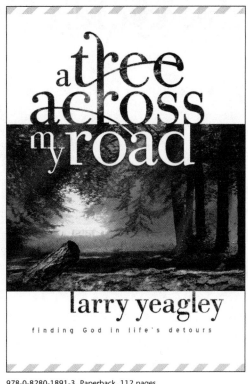

a tree across my road

larry yeagley

finding God in life's detours

978-0-8280-1891-3. Paperback, 112 pages.

## 3 Ways to Shop
- Visit your local Adventist Book Center®.
- Call 1-800-765-6955.
- Order online at www.AdventistBookCenter.com.

# Break the cycle.

Discover how to break the anger habit and experience the radical joy that comes from giving and receiving forgiveness. Packed with stories and insight, this book reveals how to make a fresh start, surrender your grudges, and be set free.

BEYOND ANGER

FINDING *the* FREEDOM *of* FORGIVENESS

LARRY YEAGLEY

978-0-8280-1943-9. Paperback, 128 pages.

# Enhance your worship program.

Tired of the cliché and predictable? Enjoy a fresh take on issues important to youth and young adults with these field-tested skits that deal with such topics as knowing God's will, prayer, dating and friendship, and authentic Christianity. The skits have designated themes and require very few props, so it's easy to incorporate drama into Sabbath school, church, camp, school worships, or vespers.

978-0-8280-1883-8. Paperback, 175 pages.

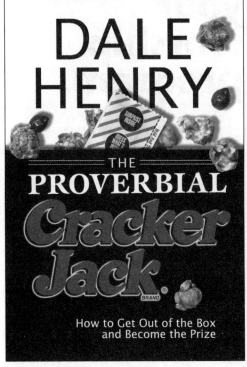